DELIBERATION

IN THE CLASSROOM

FOSTERING CRITICAL THINKING, COMMUNITY, AND CITIZENSHIP IN SCHOOLS

Stacie Molnar-Main

**KETTERING
FOUNDATION
PRESS**

PROGRAM OFFICERS: Libby Kingseed, Mindy LaBreck
COPY EDITORS: Maura Casey, Joey Easton, Jared Namenson
MANAGING EDITOR: Joey Easton
PROOFREADER: Lisa Boone-Berry
ART DIRECTION AND PRODUCTION: Laura Halsey

Deliberation in the Classroom: Fostering Critical Thinking, Community, and Citizenship in Schools is published by Kettering Foundation Press.

The interpretations and conclusions contained in this book represent the views of the author. They do not necessarily reflect the views of the Charles F. Kettering Foundation, its directors, or its officers.

For information about permission to reproduce selections from this book, write to:

Permissions
Kettering Foundation Press
200 Commons Road
Dayton, Ohio 45459

This book is printed on acid-free paper.

First edition, 2017

Manufactured in the United States of America

ISBN: 978-1-945577-06-2
Library of Congress Control Number: 2016956336

Table of Contents

APPENDICES

APPENDIX A

APPENDIX B

APPENDIX C

APPENDIX D

APPENDIX E

APPENDIX F

APPENDIX G

Acknowledgements

Deliberation in the Classroom would not have been possible without the generosity and support of many people. Educators who use deliberation and support one another's experimentation with the practice contributed to the insights I share here, and have been a constant source of inspiration to me and to one another. This book is a testament to the passion and dedication of educators like Joseph Leavy, Carmela Leonardi, Nicole Mulholland, Deborah Francis, Jon Lodge, Lori McGarry, Donnan Stoicovy, Robert Furmanek, Deb Poveromo, JohnMark Edwards, Zakiya Jenkins, Jessica Wedgeworth, Peggy Sparks, Curtis Sparks, Jacqueline Jackson, Kevin Kreig, Sarah Schneck, Tolea Kamm-Peissig, John Greenwood, Susan Miller, Carol Lee Pyfer, Phil Kane, Ken Donovan, James Gilmartin, Michael D'Innocenzo, Bernie Stein, David Huitt, Yannabah Lewis, Karen Schmidt, Simon Spelling, Barry McNealy, Brenda Guyton, Ronnie McCallum, William Medlock, Jerry Strickland, Elkin Terry Jack, John Sampson, Janice Christian, Sher'ron Hardwick, Paul Hoomes, Jerry Ingram, Wilena McCarter, Tracey Williams, Gregory Fields, Linda Givan, Tasha Gray, Latoya Posey, Christopher McCauley, Gerald Ott, and Cristina Alfaro.

I owe a debt of gratitude to the teachers and mentors who helped to cultivate my passion for civic learning and deliberation. Harris Sokoloff and Rick Battistoni were early mentors as I explored methods and practices for engaging young people as citizens in their schools and communities. Later, David Mathews taught me about community politics, and modeled the type of inquiring, listening, and learning citizenship that deliberation can engender, and Myrna Shure helped me recognize that very young children can practice deliberation if we are committed to teaching social problem solving as a developmental activity.

Deciding how to give voice to the teachers' experiences was my greatest challenge. Because I was trained in academic institutions, I was inclined to write for academic audiences. I owe thanks to Maura Casey for her expert editorial assistance in the early stages of writing this book, and to Libby Kingseed, Mindy LaBreck, Bill Muse, Etana Jacobi, John Doble, Shira Eve Epstein, and Alex Lovit for reading drafts and/or engaging in critical conversations with me. Libby's continual presence and shepherding kept me focused on the goal of creating a piece that could be easily read and digested by the public, while helping me decide when the manuscript was ready to release. In the final stages, Joey Easton provided expert copy editing and counsel, and Laura Halsey offered an attractive design that, I think, complements and strengthens the text.

Stacie Molnar-Main

Foreword

....

The Kettering Foundation is a nonprofit operating foundation rooted in the American tradition of cooperative research. Kettering's primary research question is, what does it take to make democracy work as it should? Kettering's research is distinctive in that it is conducted from the perspective of citizens and focuses on what people can do collectively to address problems that affect their lives, their communities, and their nation.

One of the problems of democracy that Kettering has identified is that many people do not pursue an active role in the decision-making life of their communities and country. They don't see their concerns represented in the politics around them; they don't think they can make a difference in solving their community's problems; and sometimes they make hasty or poor decisions about what needs to be done. Few people seem to identify roles or responsibilities for citizens other than voting and obeying laws.

The research behind *Deliberation in the Classroom* grew out of Kettering's recognition that the education of young people could include a space for them to learn about the kind of politics that will help them solve problems in their lives. The research focused on classroom teachers as one of the keys to educating young people about their roles as citizens in a democracy and teaching the practice of deliberative politics.

As a research foundation, Kettering works primarily through learning exchanges and other collaborative research with individuals, as well as civic organizations, communities, and institutions, who are experimenting with ways to strengthen democracy. The foundation learns by exchanging ideas and experiences from people and organizations who are trying to effect change in their own communities with insights that Kettering has collected from past exchanges.

From the first appearance of the National Issues Forums in 1982, Kettering became aware of teachers who recognized the usefulness of both the NIF issue guides and the process of framing issues for deliberation as models for the role and work of citizens in a democracy. In 2006, the foundation began a series of learning exchanges—known as Teaching with Deliberation—with teachers interested in using deliberation with their students. Those learning exchanges, and the reports teachers and administrators produced over the past ten years, helped identify the key benefits and challenges teachers experienced when introducing deliberative practices into their classrooms, and documented teachers' observations about the impact deliberation had on their students' sense of themselves as democratic citizens.

Deliberation in the Classroom is the product of that research. Kettering believes the book's insights, presented in terms that resonate with educators, will support both the wider use of deliberative practices and the goal of growing the number of students who recognize a role for themselves as citizens in a democracy.

Libby Kingseed, Program Officer and Archivist

Mindy LaBreck, Program Officer and
Director of Administrative Services

Kettering Foundation

Preface

....

When I began writing this book, I could not have predicted that it would be published after one of the most polarizing presidential campaigns in recent memory. The 2016 campaign and election season have given voice to perspectives that many would rather ignore, and it has uncovered deep ideological divisions in American society. It is an opportune time to be advocating for public deliberation in schools: it is clear that Americans need ways of talking and learning about public issues — ways that can bridge divides and contribute to a more informed and engaged citizenry. Yet I would be remiss if I did not acknowledge that deliberation is only one approach to practicing the active and informed citizenship that is important to our democracy and to our schools.

Deliberation in the Classroom highlights the work of educators who place civic education at the heart of their work by choosing to teach their students an alternative to the divisive, zero-sum politics advanced by interest groups and portrayed in the media. These educators embrace participatory models of learning and decision making and work hard to expose students to difficult issues and varied perspectives, including unpopular and marginalized points of view. They understand that critical thinking and community building are not mutually exclusive terms, and that citizens need to learn how to talk, listen, and work with others so they can tackle complex issues that affect their communities. These teachers understand that civic education should be nonideological, pragmatic, and rooted in democracy. While it encompasses a wide range of skills and knowledge, civic education should at least provide students with the practical skills and dispositions they need to analyze information, ask questions, build arguments, express agreement and dissent, understand others, and work across divides for the common good.

I focused on the National Issues Forums (NIF) Teachers Network because I had access to this group through my participation in a learning exchange at the

Kettering Foundation. Like the teachers who are described here, I had worked with NIF-style deliberation as an educator, and began to adapt the practice over time for different groups and settings because I saw how it contributed to powerful learning and improved engagement among citizens that deliberate together. Through involvement in the learning exchange, the teachers and I had the opportunity to share experiences, resources, and discoveries, which resulted in the stories and themes reported here.

I chose to focus on teachers' stories and practical experiences with public-issues deliberation for several reasons. First, Diana Hess, Paula McIvoy, and Walter Parker have written extensively and effectively on the theory and practice of discussion-based classrooms, ethical considerations in teaching with political issues, and the value of studying controversial public issues. In this study, I refer readers to the works of those authors and others for analyses and additional applications of discussion-based classroom techniques. There is a clear research base to guide deep work in this field, and I encourage educators to incorporate these perspectives into their reflection, planning, and practice.

Second, there is a plethora of descriptions of "effective teaching practices" that emphasize measurable outcomes, but fail to capture the significant changes that occur in classrooms and in students' lives as a result of quality teaching. *Deliberation in the Classroom* supplements research on civic education, inquiry-based classrooms, and discussion-based pedagogies with rich descriptions of the type of learning experiences that matter for students' futures and our democracy. Central to these stories are the positive relationships the teachers cultivated with their students and the supportive classroom atmosphere that undergirds meaningful civic learning. This book is a humble testimony to these dimensions of educational improvement, which are often neglected by school reformers.

Finally, I highlighted real teachers and classrooms because I wanted to provide concrete examples of how public deliberation looks, the benefits and challenges it offers, and how it has been adapted in real schools. My hope is that teachers, school administrators, and citizens might be drawn into the stories and inspired to bring deliberation to youth in their communities.

CHAPTER ONE

An Introduction to Deliberation in the Classroom

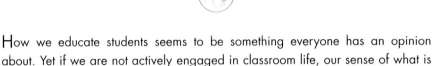

How we educate students seems to be something everyone has an opinion about. Yet if we are not actively engaged in classroom life, our sense of what is happening in schools may be limited to our own experiences or what we have seen in the media. That is why I like to listen carefully to the ways teachers, students, and parents talk about their experiences in schools. These conversations often reveal striking information about what is working in American education and where our schools may not be living up to some common ideals.

A few months before I began to write this book, I met with a group of teachers who were learning how to use historical documents from the National Archives to enrich instruction. While discussing resources and exercises they planned to use with students, the conversation took an interesting turn. The teachers began talking about what students really learn in school and how they, as teachers, struggle to make their classes relevant:

- "I think the main thing my kids learn in my school is 'how to do school.' They learn very little about what really matters in life," stated a high school special education teacher.

- An Advanced Placement (AP) American history teacher lamented that his students may be prepared for college but "they are not prepared to be citizens—to understand the system and organize to make the world a better place."

- A middle school social studies teacher noted that her students were unprepared for life because they did not know how to deal with uncertainty. "If there's not an obvious answer, my students freeze or freak out. They say the assignment isn't fair. They don't persevere . . . They definitely don't look to each other. They want me to give them the answer."

In one way or another, all three teachers had drawn similar conclusions from their very different classroom experiences. They felt that their students were learning important information and skills in school, but that public education was failing to prepare students for a complex, uncertain, and interdependent world. Each teacher felt too tied to curricula that focused on facts and contrived experiences. All yearned for more opportunities to engage students in learning about issues that matter to them and to society.

Over the years, I have had the privilege of working with many educators who teach in very different types of schools. I have concluded that it is quite common for teachers to feel a combination of pride and frustration when reflecting on their teaching and student learning. At the root of this conflict is the tension between educators' love for teaching—especially their interest in preparing students for life—and the realities of their job: exhausting schedules, scarce resources, and constraints on their autonomy. They wonder if they are doing enough to prepare students to become contributing citizens, but they are not sure what they can do differently.

Preparing All Students for Civic Life

Deliberation in the Classroom is written for educators and parents who care about public education and are looking for ways to make learning more relevant to all students, including those who are disengaged from school. It is a book for citizens who are concerned about political polarization in America[1] and who want the next generation to be prepared to participate effectively in solving the big problems of the day. And it is a story of teachers doing public work[2] by bringing public issues into their classrooms and engaging students in public deliberation about what should be done.

Before I describe more fully what public deliberation is, I want to introduce you to two teachers who use it. Jim Gilmartin and Sarah Schneck teach in very different types of schools. Yet they are both clear about what motivates them to use deliberation in the classroom.

Gilmartin chairs the social studies department and coordinates the International Baccalaureate program in the West Islip School District on Long Island. He is creative, energetic, and passionate about his work. That may be why Gilmartin makes a point of modeling teaching practices that help others get excited about learning. This is not always an easy task. Because most West Islip students are from middle-income families and are bound for college, the school focuses on preparing its students for the New York Regents Exams and college entrance tests. This reality can make it difficult to justify the use of any teaching practice that does not produce measurable results. Nevertheless, after ten years of working with deliberation, West Islip teachers and school leaders remain committed to infusing deliberation into the K-12 curriculum. Gilmartin says the school district is committed to deliberation because it changes how students think, write, and understand their roles in society. Students learn how to be critical thinkers, analyze sources, and identify biases, while also learning how to "disagree without being unlikable." These skills will help them succeed in college, in their careers, and in a global society.

Sarah Schneck teaches at the Enrich, Excel, Achieve Learning Academy (EEA), a public charter school in Wausau, Wisconsin. EEA focuses on youth who have not succeeded in a traditional school setting. Schneck's students include teen parents, students who have been truant, and youth facing other serious challenges. Most of the students come from low-income families. Schneck would be the first to tell you the term "at-risk" does not adequately describe her kids. Aside from their very different individual histories, Schneck's students, like Gilmartin's, are diverse in other ways. Some are disruptive. Some are shy. Some are animated. Some are depressed. Some are struggling academically; others are not. All of them will be able to vote someday, and will live and work in communities with others.

Schneck believes it is impossible for teachers to really teach kids without understanding what students need to be successful in community life. Teachers need to prepare youth to deal with complexity, to work with others, and to resolve conflict. She says, "I think we have a job, as educators, to not teach kids *what* to think. We need to teach them *how* to think." That includes teaching students how to think *with* others, especially those who have different views and experiences than they do.

Gilmartin and Schneck see their work as a calling—something more than a job. They believe teachers have an obligation to students and to society. That is why they spend time preparing students for democratic citizenship as well as state tests. The type of democratic citizenship they emphasize has little to do with voting, service, or protest (although these have their place in democracy). It is a citizenship of community building, colearning, and collective action, supported by a process known as public deliberation.

Deliberation in the Classroom

Public deliberation is a form of discussion used by many communities to engage diverse groups of citizens in work to address community problems.[3] In the classroom, deliberation is a learning process that has six key characteristics:

1. The focus or topic of learning is an issue of significance to individuals and society.[4]

2. The learning is highly interactive and discussion based.

3. Teachers and students share responsibility for learning.

4. The process emphasizes weighing options or deciding.

5. Multiple perspectives, including marginalized views, are given balanced consideration.[5]

6. Students are treated as citizens or decision makers, often engaging in follow-up activities related to these roles.

In classrooms where public deliberation is practiced, learners engage in inquiry about complex issues and participate in deliberative discussions. During deliberative discussions, students consider different perspectives on a social problem, identify and work through tensions related to different approaches to addressing the problem, and attempt to arrive at reasoned judgment together. In contrast to processes that encourage consensus or compromise, the goal of deliberation is not to produce complete agreement among participants. The broad goals, among other curricular goals, are to promote improved understanding of the issue, awareness of the consequences of various responses, and recognition of commonly held values that can inform future action.

"I think we have a job, as educators, to not teach kids what to think. We need to teach them how to think." - Sarah Schneck

Teachers can use deliberation in the classroom in many different ways to meet a range of objectives. This book presents stories of educators who use deliberation to support teaching and learning about contemporary issues. It describes how others use deliberation to enrich their teaching of historic decisions, and provides examples of how teachers use deliberation to teach communication, critical thinking, and noncognitive skills like empathy. Students, in turn, show improvements in their abilities to think, talk, and write about complex ideas and controversial topics, and develop a deeper awareness of their roles as citizens of a democracy.

Education and the Public Good

There are many reasons why American youth should practice deliberation. For me, the importance of teaching students explicitly how to engage with difficult public issues was reinforced by the Charlie Hebdo attacks of January 7, 2015. On that day, Islamic extremists entered the offices of a French satirical magazine and gunned down security workers and cartoonists for their role in mocking the Prophet Muhammad. One of the victims was a Muslim. He and the attackers had all been educated in France—a country that protects free speech and espouses democratic ideals. Like many people, I doubted anything could have been done to prevent the tragedy or redirect the life course of the murderers. Extremism is insidious, and violence can seem irrational.

Then, I read a *New York Times* commentary written by Abdelkader Benali. In it, he described what it was like to grow up as a Muslim in a Western society. Despite having family traditions that differed from those of his peers, Benali identified with his country and felt connected to his school and classmates until a fateful day when a high school teacher muddled through a class discussion about the *fatwa* against Salman Rushdie. As Benali explains, the conversation occurred with

The educators I describe are committed to engaging students with public issues and teaching students how to discuss challenging topics with civility and a critical lens.

little context, and the students in his class were perplexed by the notion of *fatwa*. As the only Muslim in the room, Benali attempted to explain the significance of insulting the Prophet within his religion. His teacher argued that it was irrational for someone to be offended by fiction: "How could using one's imagination lead to a death sentence?"[6] Benali grew angry and was eventually dismissed from class.

The experience in Benali's class was the first time he really understood how extreme or separatist ideologies could take root in young people. While most teens feel "different" or outcast at times, these feelings can be reinforced or exacerbated in schools where teachers are not skilled at facilitating conversations about controversial topics that naturally emerge in their classrooms. When these experiences coincide with a political culture in which groups of people feel mocked or suppressed, teens who feel marginalized may be at risk of disengaging with school or civil society altogether, according to Benali.

I believe Benali's teacher had good intentions in trying to bring current events into his classroom. Students tend to be interested in discussing topics from the media, and research suggests learning improves when students are engaged. Indeed, many notable civic-education programs foster youth engagement with the news and public issues as a way of promoting civic literacy.[7] The problem was in how Benali's teacher approached the topic of *fatwa*, and how he engaged students in discussion of it. Rather than promoting learning about diverse perspectives, the teacher only allowed room in the conversation for his own opinions about the Muslim faith. Instead of empowering all students to pose questions, engage in clarifying or critical thinking, and discuss the relevance of the topic to the curriculum, some students' voices were elevated over others, one student was alienated from his classmates and his country, and opportunities for reinforcing civic skills and academic learning were lost.[8]

Although public issues, such as political extremism, immigration, and other topics, can provide a rich and motivating context for student learning, this example demonstrates why some teachers want to avoid these issues, not discuss them with their students, and stay focused on the planned curriculum. Others feel they don't have time, or the expertise, to address such complicated topics in their classroom. Still, many teachers have a sense that current events and public issues present teachable moments and opportunities for enduring lessons to be learned. They want to know how to facilitate and frame conversations to ensure that students are learning the intended academic content and skills while also being exposed to differing perspectives and gaining insight about citizenship and challenges to democracy.

The educators I describe here, including Gilmartin and Schneck, are committed to engaging students with public issues and teaching students how to discuss challenging topics with civility and a critical lens. They are less interested in directing students to "one right answer" than they are in teaching students to talk across differences, understand different viewpoints, and learn how to act as citizens when presented with complex problems and an unclear path forward.

The teachers have been a part of a professional development network focused on using deliberation in the K-12 classroom. The network, known as the National Issues Forums (NIF) Teachers Network, was convened by local partners in four communities: Birmingham, Alabama; Wausau, Wisconsin; Long Island, New York; and State College, Pennsylvania. As part of this network, teachers worked with colleagues to integrate deliberation into their classrooms using resources published by the National Issues Forums Institute (NIFI).[9]

Deliberation in the Classroom describes the experiences of some of the teachers in the NIF Teachers Network, and what they learned from those experiences. It answers questions like, What does deliberation in the classroom look like in comparison to other forms of learning? How does it affect students, and how is learning measured? It explores how teachers are working to address students' individual learning needs while also meeting the needs of our democracy. Finally, it describes some of the challenges educators face in teaching with deliberation, as well as the types of support communities and school leaders can provide to advance this type of teaching and reclaim the civic mission of public schools.

CHAPTER TWO

Why Teach Deliberation?

I am often asked why deliberation is such an important thing for children to experience in school. One answer is simple. Children are citizens too, and deliberation allows them to practice important skills of citizenship while engaging with issues that are relevant to their communities and democracy. Another answer relates to the state of politics in America: in today's media environment, it is quite possible that a child could grow up without experiencing an example of democratic politics in which people of different viewpoints work together for the common good. By teaching with deliberation, educators model a way of talking about public issues that enables diverse students to learn together, identify common ground, and connect their learning to civic action.

Rationales for teaching with deliberation are rooted in deliberative democratic theory. The basic premise is that democracy functions more effectively when many sources of information are brought to bear on public decision making and decision-making processes are transparent and open to anyone affected by the decision.[10] Although issues like bullying, quality education, and addiction affect young people, most students rarely engage in the decision-making processes that inform local problem solving or public policy about these issues. By teaching with deliberation, teachers can provide students with an opportunity to assume an active role in learning about and addressing school, community, or national issues. In this process, students also:

- learn content and make personal connections to issues;

- learn about others' concerns and experiences;

- argue for and evaluate different approaches to a problem;

- practice expressing agreement and disagreement;

- learn how to find common ground with those who have different views and experiences;

- maintain their own views about the issue, which may differ from those of others in the class.

The type of civic education engendered by deliberation is particularly suitable for a diverse democracy because, when it occurs within a classroom where young people feel safe to express themselves, students can develop knowledge, tolerance for others' views, and an expanded view of the role of citizens in a democracy.[11] When students deliberate about historical issues, they develop historical empathy and an awareness of the experiences of diverse historical actors, including everyday citizens.

Outcomes such as these have led groups concerned about civic education to endorse deliberation as an important K-12 instructional strategy. The National Conference on Citizenship and the Campaign for the Civic Mission of Schools recommend that students have opportunities to discuss current events and controversial issues in school as a way of promoting informed and active citizenship.[12] Deliberation is also defined within the National Council for the Social Studies' *C3 Framework for Social Studies State Standards*[13] as a supportive process for teaching students how to communicate conclusions and take informed action. The connection between deliberation and citizenship is well stated within the NCSS *C3 Framework*:

> Active and responsible citizens identify and analyze public problems; deliberate with other people about how to define and address issues; take constructive, collaborative action; reflect on their actions; create and sustain groups; and influence institutions both large and small.[14]

This definition of active and responsible citizenship reminds us that civic education is hefty work that should be directed at producing more than citizens who can vote. It should support the development of citizens who can participate critically and creatively in public life through work with others and by influencing the institutions of democracy.

Habits of Mind and Accountable Talk

A deliberative approach to teaching and learning can support students' civic development in an integrated way, allowing teachers to attend to their academic goals for students while also helping students develop as citizen-learners. For most teachers in the NIF network, civic learning was a welcomed side effect of their work with deliberation. When they began experimenting with the practice, most were interested in using deliberation to teach academic content. American history teachers, for example, used NIF materials and deliberations to teach about issues surrounding the Declaration of Independence and the Constitutional Convention. Global studies teachers used issue guides on immigration and America's role in the world to reinforce curricular themes and introduce American perspectives on globalization. Biology teachers used issue guides on environmental topics to illustrate the connections between ecology standards and local and national policies.

Over time, teachers began to see ways that deliberation could be used to extend their curricula and connect it to rigorous academic standards for reading, writing, speaking, and listening. Deliberation also provided opportunities for teachers to observe and foster students' critical-thinking skills in the context of classroom discussions that require students to reason aloud, listen to others, and improve their collective thinking. When people can think flexibly about a problem, pose questions, and engage interdependently, they can behave intelligently in the face of complex problems, according to Arthur Costa and Bena Kallick. These *habits of mind*, if employed with intention, enable students to respond to situations in ways that increase the likelihood of a successful outcome and help them keep learning.[15]

When teachers use deliberation in the classroom, students exercise many of the habits of mind associated with successful learning and problem solving. For example, students who learn with deliberation *apply past knowledge to new situations* as they learn new vocabulary, information, and perspectives related to the issues they are studying. In preparation for deliberation, students also study different approaches to understanding public problems and consider the benefits and trade-offs of different strategies. These experiences teach students how to *think flexibly* and *ask questions* to discern the strengths and weaknesses of different choices. When students eventually deliberate in class, they engage in rigorous conversations with their peers and are encouraged by their teachers to *think interdependently and communicate with clarity and precision.*

When students deliberate, they are expected to listen and respond to classmates in ways that expose new information and perspectives, clarify thinking, and promote improved understanding among the group. Researchers call this type of engagement academically productive classroom talk or "accountable talk." It is a form of learning in which students are accountable to each other, to accepted standards of reasoning, and to the subject about which they are learning.[16] Research shows classrooms where academically productive talk is the norm can promote achievement among students with differing economic backgrounds, cultures, and languages.[17] When applied in a systemic way, accountable talk can lead to improved academic rigor in classrooms and in entire schools.[18]

Social and Noncognitive Skills

Of course, students need to possess more than reasoning skills to be successful in life. They also need to develop interpersonal skills like communicating well with others, and intrapersonal skills, such as self-discipline and the ability to cope with change. These skills enable students to work better in groups, adapt to new situations, and persevere in the face of challenges.[19] Teachers who use deliberation in the classroom report that the practice helps students become more engaged and motivated in class, and it improves students' ability to communicate, empathize with others, and solve problems with people of diverse backgrounds and experiences. These types of noncognitive skills[20] help students succeed in life and careers, according to a number of recent studies.[21]

That deliberation helps students develop such skills might come as a surprise. After all, conversations about controversial public issues are fraught with opportunities for conflict and gridlock. Yet in classes that deliberate regularly, students learn to talk across these differences. They learn to identify how individuals' opinions and world views relate to things held commonly valuable within a community, such as the desire to live in safety or be treated fairly. As students discuss the best-case argument for different solutions, they come to understand others' perspectives, and often respond with empathy. They not only practice the skills of listening, speaking, and disagreeing respectfully, but they also learn an approach to problem solving that prepares them to find common ground amid differences.

Research on decision making suggests adolescents may be particularly suited to benefit from activities like public deliberation. This is because deliberation engages two distinct forms of cognition that develop during adolescence, and

Conversations about controversial public issues are fraught with opportunities for conflict. Yet in classes that deliberate regularly, students learn to talk across these differences.

which underlie human decision making: the "reasoned pathway" and the "social reaction pathway."[22] The former is based in "conscious, deliberate evaluation of costs and benefits of choice alternatives" and the latter is "grounded in experiential processes," according to psychologists Dustin Albert and Laurence Steinberg.[23] As children mature, both decision-making pathways evolve and contribute to the development of habits of mind that aid in decision-making processes. During childhood and adolescence, people are particularly prone to use social content impulsively, in ways that can reinforce stereotypes and limit the range of actions considered in decision making, research suggests. The dual role of rational and experiential thinking is believed to account, in part, for why some young people choose to engage in risky behavior and others do not, and why some youth are better able to bounce back after challenges.

Social and noncognitive factors play a role in risk and resiliency too. Specifically, individuals who possess decision-making skills, interpersonal skills, and an awareness of self and others experience fewer negative life outcomes than people who do not possess these skills.[24] Students with these skills also do better in school, according to a recent meta-analysis.[25] Unfortunately, some educators believe they cannot spend time teaching these skills because of the demands of a full curriculum and the consequences of not performing on high-stakes tests.

Deliberation provides teachers with a way to reinforce noncognitive skills in the context of academic learning. Teachers in the NIF network conveyed many powerful stories of how they used deliberation to teach academic skills, while also influencing their students' motivation, relationships, and approach to problem solving. For example, Barry McNealy, a teacher from Birmingham, wrote about the effects of deliberation on Jasmine,[26] a student known for being tough and confrontational. After a deliberative forum on youth violence, in which students discussed the impact of violence in the community and weighed different approaches to addressing violence, Jasmine came to class and announced that she had just avoided a confrontation in the hallway. "I walked away because of what we talked about in our forum," she stated.

While Jasmine had always known there were alternatives to violence, she said the forum motivated her to change her behavior. After listening to the perspectives of other students, she understood how others felt about violence and how her choices could affect the school and community.

Raymond, a senior at West Islip High School, described how deliberation improved the quality of his relationships. For him, however, the effects extended beyond school. According to Raymond, "Deliberation gives me something to talk about with my dad and another way of dealing with controversy." After being introduced to deliberation at school, Raymond says he came to see the strengths of different points of view on issues like gun violence and immigration. He also developed a skill set for talking about these ideas with his parents and other adults. "It has really improved our relationship. My parents treat me more like a grown-up when they see I have ideas about things that I have thought through."

The students who experienced deliberation demonstrated a capacity to handle complex topics, consider multiple perspectives, and identify trade-offs associated with different solutions to a problem.

Citizen Development

The type of decision making Jasmine and Raymond learned emphasizes what people hold valuable—the essence of many social and political conflicts. Rather than approaching decision making as a simple matter of weighing pros and cons and identifying the choice with the most positive attributes, deliberation provides a way for citizens to deal with problems that are messy and hard to handle, but that have real implications for individuals and the community. These problems are often referred to as "wicked problems"[27] because they have numerous potential causes and solutions, their solutions evoke competing values, and institutions and individuals must engage in sustained action in order to effect change.

While wicked problems like poverty, community violence, and the national debt are real and consequential in communities and in the lives of individuals, it is common for citizens to feel like these problems are out of their grasp. Yet a strong democracy depends on the ability of citizens and policymakers to grapple with difficult issues and act in ways to move society to a better place.

Experience with deliberation in the classroom can increase students' confidence and skills in dealing with complex public issues, research suggests. Two qualitative studies demonstrate this. The first study[28] compared students who were exposed to public deliberation as a central practice in a high school course to students who had not experienced deliberation. Students from each group were given scenarios that included wicked problems, and then they were asked to propose a public response. The researchers observed the students as they planned their response. They also interviewed some participants to learn about their experiences. According to the researchers, the students who experienced deliberation in the classroom demonstrated a capacity to handle complex topics, consider multiple perspectives, and identify trade-offs associated with different solutions to a problem. They also demonstrated the ability to listen and talk with others in ways that furthered the group's work toward developing a reasonable plan to address the issue. This included reframing the issue to include diverse perspectives when the definition of the problem did not include some peoples' voices. In contrast, students who had not been taught in classrooms that use deliberation struggled to develop a response to most scenarios. Though all participants in the study were successful students, the groups that had not experienced deliberation were "virtually paralyzed, unable to get a handle on the issue, and unsure how to begin addressing the problem,"[29] researchers reported.

Another study, conducted at Wake Forest University, compared a group of college students who were taught by incorporating public deliberation to a control group of Wake Forest students over a four-year period.[30] The students who experienced deliberation in the classroom, known as Democracy Fellows, attended classes that included deliberative experiences, learned to research and develop resources to support deliberation, and hosted deliberative forums on campus. Throughout the students' years at Wake Forest, they were interviewed individually and in focus groups convened by the researchers. They also completed surveys that asked them to describe their political involvement and attitudes.

While the Democracy Fellows and the control group were alike in most regards at the onset of the study, distinctions emerged over time. Students who were exposed to deliberation became more aware of the responsibilities of active citizenship, and were more apt to vote, volunteer for a political campaign, and communicate with elected officials. They also demonstrated the ability to reason about public issues in sophisticated and nuanced ways, using analysis and critical thinking. Finally, Democracy Fellows expressed confidence in their ability to participate in solving public problems, and could imagine many different ways of working with others for the common good. The control group, in contrast, was less confident in dealing with controversial public issues, and recognized fewer options for citizen action. In a ten-year follow-up study, differences between the Democracy Fellows and control group persisted. Specifically, Fellows expressed a more complex view of citizenship, a willingness to talk with people who don't share their beliefs, and a view that they can have a say in what government does.[31]

These findings get to the heart of why it is important to teach deliberation. More than most other teaching strategies, deliberation prepares students to grapple with public problems as citizens, and it empowers students to envision many different actions and roles they can take in their community—and in our democracy—to make a difference.

Why Does America Need More Educators Who Teach Public Deliberation?

The types of lessons and skills learned from public deliberation are important for students and for society. Students need to know how to read, write, and speak to succeed in school and work. They need to know how to analyze information, think critically, and work with others to excel in their roles. And society needs more citizens who can talk and work across divides to solve the problems our communities face. Unfortunately, trends suggest that our nation may be moving further away from this democratic ideal, and the stakes may be highest for disadvantaged students.

In his book on demographic and political trends in American society, Bill Bishop[32] presented compelling evidence that, in the past thirty years, Americans have become increasingly segregated and isolated within like-minded factions. This is reflected in the growing homogeneity of political party registrations in voting districts, as well as in the choices people make about where they worship, where they shop, and where they congregate, in person and online. The result of this "big sort," as Bishop calls it, is that the ideological divides between the political parties and among citizens has grown. People are more likely to live and socialize exclusively in communities with people who think like they do about a range of issues. They are also reluctant to engage in political conversations with people who may have different political views.[33]

This type of sorting is consequential for America and its future. When people only interact with individuals who share their views and experiences, they are less likely to be exposed to information that challenges those views and aspects of their thinking that may be faulty. They are also more likely to misunderstand the values, motivations, and characteristics of people who are different from themselves. This creates the conditions for polarizing and divisive characterizations of political issues (and opponents) and contributes to a public that is more self-oriented than public oriented. The result is a citizenry that is less likely to work across social divides to address all kinds of public problems, including those that the government cannot address.

Because deliberation can promote the very skills and dispositions citizens need to work across divides, it can prepare students to work together in the face of deep-seated differences. Unfortunately, many American students do not have access to the types of civic-oriented classes that support the development of these skills.[34] Research suggests this is especially true for nonwhite youth and youth attending low-socioeconomic status schools.[35]

Thus, the case for teaching deliberation is straightforward. It is about supporting a stronger democracy by ensuring the next generation of citizens has the skills needed to act on the pressing issues facing our nation and communities. It is about teaching all children how to move beyond individual mind-sets to engage in collective reasoning, and about nurturing important civic skills in all classrooms. This involves teaching academic skills and more. It is about embracing the civic mission of K-12 education, while committing to educate the whole citizen-student in the laboratory of public life.

CHAPTER THREE

Engaging Citizen-Students

In many American schools, student populations—like the demographics of the nation—are transforming rapidly. This is certainly true at Huntington Union Free School District on Long Island, New York, where 45 percent of students are economically disadvantaged, most are nonwhite, and 12.5 percent are English Language Learners (ELL).[36] Joe Leavy, chair of the humanities department, sees Huntington High School as a microcosm of America. Its student population includes wealthier students from Huntington Bay and poorer students living in Huntington Station.

Culturally and linguistically, the district is increasingly diverse, and this has made changing demographics a touchy issue in the community. At times, resentment has flared at public meetings, where vocal citizens have questioned the attention given to new Americans and the dollars spent educating students who may not be documented residents. Teachers in the school have avoided getting mired in the issue. Most teachers believe "kids are kids," according to Leavy. "We have an obligation to teach all kids, regardless of immigration status."

Huntington High School is the type of school district targeted by legislative efforts to leave no child behind. It educates students from many different socioeconomic and cultural communities, allowing school and state officials to shine a light on how subgroups of students are performing. Although Huntington is a successful school in many regards, its special-education students and students with limited English proficiency have not done as well on accountability tests as other groups. As a result, the school district has faced tough choices in recent years concerning what to teach and how to optimize student learning.

Carmela Leonardi, retired principal of Huntington High School, was deeply involved in the district's strategy to improve the achievement of all students. Unlike most high school principals who spent their careers in secondary education,

Leonardi led an elementary and an intermediate school in the same district before taking the helm at the high school. This experience gave her a unique perspective on where her students come from and what they need to succeed:

> If you tell me my school is a focus school (because ELL students' test scores are not high enough), I don't get upset. It tells me we have work to do. Many of our students come to us with disrupted educational experiences or they have not been prepared for this level of work. We need to work with these students and we need to give them what they need.

For Leonardi, giving struggling learners what they need does not mean narrowing the curriculum or limiting students' access to complex ideas and discussion. At her school, ELL students are afforded an extra year in high school to learn basic skills if they need it. They are also fully integrated into challenging classes, where teachers focus on asking higher-order questions and challenging them to think.

"What we need are more students who are pests— the ones you can't keep quiet, the ones who keep asking the questions."
- Carmela Leonardi

Leonardi is a strong supporter of deliberation because she understands the value of teaching students how to question others and think critically about information they encounter. This perspective, she contends, is rooted in her own story of immigration. At sixteen, Leonardi entered the United States public school system after being raised in Italy under a totally different model of education. Prior to coming to the United States, she had been taught that, "the teacher had all the information. All I had to do was do what the teacher wanted me to do." Leonardi was transfixed and transformed when she entered school in the United States. "Students were questioning everything, even their teachers. I was intimidated by this at first, but then it got to me. I started asking questions. Then, I could not be stopped. I questioned everything."

She attributes her success as a leader to what she learned in American schools: how to listen critically, ask effective questions, and push for answers in the face of challenges—hallmarks of an American education that may be slipping away due to the over-emphasis on standardized test scores. She wants all students in Huntington to have a similar educational experience to the one she had in American schools. She wants her school to empower students to become active citizens and leaders. "Too many kids and teachers are getting the idea that learning is about performance," she said. "What we need are more students who are pests—the ones you can't keep quiet, the ones who keep asking the questions." That is why Leonardi encourages teachers in her school to teach about public issues and experiment with discussion-based strategies like deliberation.

Engaging Learners

Leonardi's experience highlights an often ignored ingredient associated with closing the gap between high achievers and other students: the quality of students' classroom engagement is closely linked with students' motivation to learn and academic achievement.[37] Students who find schoolwork "meaningful, valuable, and worthy of one's effort" are more likely to benefit from learning activities and persist in the face of academic challenges.[38] Positive engagement is also supported in classrooms where teachers create a positive emotional climate and integrate students' perspectives into learning activities.[39]

Unfortunately, classroom engagement and achievement motivation are not a given in American classrooms. Research indicates engagement tends to decrease as students move from elementary to secondary school and as a function of the task orientation of the classroom.[40] When grades and test performance are emphasized more than the process of learning, and when students fail to see the relevance of course content, engagement suffers.[41]

Leonardi had an awakening of sorts when she learned to participate critically in class discussions. After spending years in a system focused on test performance, she experienced a new way of engaging socially and intellectually in learning when she entered classrooms where teachers valued critical analysis and inquiry. People who observe public deliberation in classrooms witness a similar transformation as students begin to make connections between problems they experience in their lives and what they are learning in school. For example, one Alabama teacher reported that she saw "increased class participation" during deliberative forums. "Students who normally declined to put forth the effort in class began to participate in discussions."

Many educators who participate in the NIF Teachers Network have observed a similar transformation in student engagement when they introduced deliberation into their classes. Some comments included:

> I expected the deliberation to be very quiet with students looking to one another for input, but to my surprise, everyone was so willing to provide their opinions. Also, I expected them to look to me to carry the conversation. Some students opened up and shared personal experiences and were willing to continue to share. . . . To have some of my shyest students open up was wonderful and surprising.

> The students that were usually less likely to participate in class were more involved, the ones that usually were in their own world were more attentive, and the leaders of the class were more followers.

> It seemed as if the shy ones were the most vocal. [Deliberation] allowed all of my students to be recognized, to have a sense of worth.

Students who rarely participate in class are often eager to join discussions about controversial issues. If the teacher encourages these types of discussions in the context of an open class climate—one in which students feel safe to explore issues and express their views without fear of judgment—students are more likely to learn to think critically about issues[42] and develop civic skills and dispositions like perspective-taking and tolerance,[43] according to research. This type of student engagement opens the door to other forms of learning. Once students connect to an issue and know their voices are valued, their interest in the topic can be channeled into academic tasks like reading, researching, and writing.

Planning to Engage All Learners

Teachers who use deliberation in the classroom are responsible for making sure students are learning the intended information and skills, while ensuring the class does not devolve into a partisan debate. This balancing act requires that teachers understand the goals of public deliberation in the classroom, have an awareness of how their own biases can undermine an open classroom climate, and take steps to ensure they are building the type of classroom community that can foster open communication, inquiry, and democratic learning.[44] This involves using class resources and activities that support the goals of deliberation prioritized by the teacher (see Table 3a).

Accomplishing this begins with carefully selecting an issue for study. Then, teachers need to present the issue in a way that allows students to see beyond binary framings of the problem (such as liberal versus conservative) and carefully weigh different options as they decide what should be done.

Trade-offs are things that must be sacrificed if a particular strategy is pursued or public decision is made. They are often connected to things people hold valuable.

Not all topics are suited to deliberation.[45] Pollution, for example, cannot be deliberated about because there is no choice to be made. Pollution is pollution. It is a fact. What you can deliberate about is how to respond to the problem of pollution and its affects on humans. This topic is suitable for deliberation because it is complex and entangled with other issues, such as regulation and health care. It is also a problem that cannot be resolved by individuals or legislators alone: it requires individuals to take action in their daily lives, and it requires a public response.

At Huntington High School and other schools featured in this work, teachers use National Issues Forums (NIF) issue guides or locally developed resources to frame how issues are studied and discussed. (See Appendix A for a sample NIF Historic

Decisions issue guide and Appendix B for a public issue framed by a nonprofit consortium, in partnership with local educators.) These issue guides[46] or issue frameworks present the issue from three distinct perspectives that differ from how the problem tends to be framed by experts or policymakers. Each perspective presents a different view of the nature of the problem and suggests specific actions that may be taken to address the issue. While NIF resources include issue-specific vocabulary and address the key points experts make, the texts are written in *citizens' terms*: they reference things that are valuable to everyday people, such as personal security, fairness, and obligations to family or community.[47]

Table 3a: Some Goals of Public Deliberation in the Classroom

Promote students' participation in discussion and reflection on the issue, including students who may be reluctant to participate.

Develop specific civic skills in students, including the ability to analyze information about public issues, recognize trade-offs associated with different policy options, find common ground with those who share different points of view, and identify actions citizens can take to address issues in their community.

Develop specific communication skills in students, such as the ability to listen, reflect on what others have said, disagree respectfully, and articulate a position or argument.

Foster interpersonal dispositions and skills, like perspective taking, empathy, and tolerance.

Connect public issues to academic content in ways that enrich and extend student learning.

Framing problems in citizens' terms is an effective way to bring people into conversations about public issues.[48] This is because experts and citizens tend to speak in "different tongues"—one highly technical and focused on data, the other relational and focused on experience. When information and issues are described in technical terms with expert-framed solutions, citizens have difficulty connecting to the conversation and may drop out because they feel ill equipped to deal with the issue, or because they believe their perspective is being ignored. By framing issues in language that highlights things held valuable to people, citizens are drawn into the conversation and are able to recognize their concerns and the concerns of others while relating to expert knowledge in new ways.

Framing public issues in citizens' terms has a similar effect on students. Many students can identify with complex ideas when the information is linked to things they have experienced or that matter to them. Some students, however, require support in connecting to the issue. For these students, it can be helpful if the teacher provides instigating content or experiences[49] to facilitate their connection to the topic. Materials like political cartoons, provocative editorials, short films, and literature with themes related to the issue can help bring the topic to life and set the stage for deliberative units.

Deliberative Forums in the Classroom: A Common Process

Joe Leavy and his colleagues at Huntington High School began their work with deliberation in the classroom by using a process known as a deliberative forum. It is the same process that citizens who participate in NIF forums experience when they gather to deliberate about public issues that affect the nation and their community. The goal of the process, for citizens, is to explore the benefits and costs of various options for addressing a public issue, discuss the trade-offs that are inherent in each choice, and determine if there is any common ground for action among the group.

The physical arrangement of a classroom forum sets the stage for group learning. Rather than sitting in rows or at tables, students sit in one large circle or smaller group circles. The teacher may sit in the circle or stand off to the side, structuring students' learning by guiding questions or by assigning a group facilitator to moderate the deliberation. After an opening statement about the goals of deliberation and a short introduction to the issue, the teacher or a student facilitator prompts the class with a personal-stake question like, "Why does this issue matter to you and to people you know?" If the class is deliberating about how to respond to community violence, for instance, students may describe how violence has affected them or their community. If deliberating about the future of Social Security or another national topic, students may describe how the issue has affected loved ones or friends. Students listen and share their reasons for caring about the topic with little intervention from the teacher.

Once students connect to the issue, the facilitator presents several approaches to understanding the problem using an issue guide or framework that describes three options or approaches to address the topic at hand. The facilitator focuses the group on one approach at a time, posing questions to guide the discussion, asking students what appeals to them about the option and prompting them to consider trade-offs associated with each approach. Trade-offs are things that must be sacrificed if a particular strategy is pursued or policy decision is made. They are often connected to things people hold valuable, and help students understand why reasonable people may hold different views about the same issue.

Phrases that pepper the conversation during forums should make it clear that students are listening to each other and considering how others' views relate to their own. If students get off task, or one student begins to dominate the discussion, the facilitator can redirect the group by asking a focusing question or referring to the ground rules for deliberation, which are typically reviewed or developed at the beginning of the forum (see Table 3b).

Table 3b: Examples of Ground Rules for Deliberation*

NIF Ground Rules (www.nifi.org)	**Guidelines for Deliberation** (Used by the Wisconsin Institute for Public Policy and Service Teachers Institute)
Everyone is encouraged to participate. No one or two individuals dominate. The discussion will focus on the choices. All the major choices or positions on the issue are considered. An atmosphere for discussion and analysis of the alternatives is maintained. We listen to each other.	Listen respectfully to different viewpoints, thoughts, and feelings. Right to pass. Value evidence variety - Learning styles - Sources of facts - Cultural attitudes and differences Seek understanding, not persuasion. We are doing choice work, where we will be making decisions about trade-offs— what we are willing to give up if we make a certain choice. We are not here to choose one of the approaches, but to consider ideas from all approaches, and create new ideas and approaches.

* Other examples of ground rules for deliberation can be found on the National Coalition for Dialogue and Deliberation website (NCDD.org).

Once the group has considered each approach, the facilitator poses a few direct questions to encourage individual and group reflection (see Table 3c). These questions are designed to help students think about how their own perspective may have changed in light of what they learned or heard during the deliberative forum. The questions also focus students' attention on the group process and the learning that may have occurred among participants. Common ground for action may emerge at this phase. Common ground refers to areas of agreement or concern, as well as any shared sense of direction that participants identify.[50]

The deliberative forum concludes with the teacher asking students to complete an authentic assignment that involves acting upon what they learned. At this point, it becomes clear that students were engaged in more than talk. They are expected to decide what should be done about the problem and act as citizens.

Table 3c: Questions to Promote Deliberation, and Reflection After Deliberation

Questions to Promote Deliberation (for each option):

What is appealing about this choice?
OR
What are the main reasons some citizens support this option?

What concerns you about this option?
OR
What concerns might other citizens have about this choice?

If this approach were adopted, what would we be giving up?
OR
What concerns would we be ignoring?

Questions to Promote Group Reflection:

Can we identify any shared sense of purpose or direction?

Can we identify any trade-offs we are, or are not, willing to make in order to move in a shared direction?

Source: Adapted from nifi.org

Students as Civic Actors

When teachers select resources to supplement students' study of public issues, they should look for materials that are related to the issue framework, according to teachers in the NIF network. By helping students recognize that much of the information that is publicly available about issues is framed in a particular way to support a particular agenda or conclusion, teachers can help students become better consumers of media and political communications. Eventually, students can learn to frame and reframe issues themselves. This skill empowers them to influence discussions and problem solving in their community.

Such was the case at Huntington High School. After taking Joe Leavy's semester-long Participation in Government course (which included three different deliberative forums), two students decided to use deliberation to address concerns about the school's code of conduct. Prior to the forum, Huntington students had been complaining about policies they felt were too constraining for high-school-aged youth. In response, Leavy's students decided to interview peers to expose concerns about the code of conduct and identify themes underlying their concerns. From there, the students framed the issue and published a two-page document that offered three different approaches for improving the school's approach to students' rights and responsibilities. The three approaches emphasized:

- Provide Developmentally Appropriate Opportunities for All: extend reasonable privileges associated with grade level to all students (Approach 1);

- Reward Responsible Behavior: link privileges to students' academic choices (Approach 2);

- Link Privileges to Contexts: extend specific rights/privileges to students in different settings of the school (Approach 3).

Each option was described in a few paragraphs and included actions, steps, and a policy proposal. Within each option, some strengths and trade-offs were highlighted.

The students' forum on the "Code of Conduct" was held after school, and was advertised in classes and on the morning announcements. Approximately thirty students attended the forum, several of whom had been disciplined under the existing code. Those students attended the meeting to make their voices heard and object to the consequences they had faced. Students from Leavy's Participation in

Government class also attended. These students had a meta-view of deliberation and were curious to see how it played out in a real-life scenario. The school principal and assistant principal were also present. These adults validated the students' efforts and heartily joined the deliberation.

Leavy's students had arranged seats in a circle and taped large blank sheets of paper to the wall for recording participants' ideas. Once everyone was seated, the students reviewed the ground rules and posed a personal-stake question to the group: "What concerns you about the student code of conduct?" Then, the deliberation began, with the student convenors acting as facilitators.

The beginning wasn't promising. The deliberation began as a heated conversation that could have easily grown out of control, according to Leavy and an assistant principal who attended the forum. The students who had come to the forum to complain were vocal in protesting the school's cell-phone policy. Other participants listened and, at times, agreed. But instead of focusing on one aspect of the issue, the student facilitators were effective in moving the conversation along—encouraging consideration of other concerns, such as the library usage policy, the dress code, and homeroom expectations. Over time, students and adults began to talk about the cell-phone issue as part of a larger constellation of concerns and possible solutions. The forum concluded with an agreement between students and the school principal to continue the conversation by convening a committee to address student privileges in the context of the code of student conduct. The assistant principal who had observed the forum was impressed by the work students had done. In reflecting on the process, he noted that students "maturely presented the issue, with solutions that were realistically understood. . . . They recognized that any choice had benefits and drawbacks." He now believes deliberation should be used more widely to engage students in problem solving about issues that affect the school.

When students take the initiative to lead forums in their community, they are engaged in a form of authentic learning—learning that "challenges students to solve everyday problems in real-world contexts."[51] It is the type of learning that proponents of the Common Core Standards and 21st Century Skills advocate.[52] Yet it does not happen by accident. It is the result of educators making intentional choices about what to teach, how to teach it, and how to assess learning.

Authentic civic learning happens in places that allow students to ask challenging questions and extend their learning beyond the classroom doors. Because the teachers and administrators at Huntington were willing to allow students to take on a controversial issue that affected the school community, the student convenors learned how to research a public issue, organize ideas to promote public problem solving, and facilitate a deliberative public meeting. Student participants in the forum learned about different approaches to improving the code of conduct, heard teachers' and principals' concerns, and experienced an alternative to the polarizing style of debate that often dominates the news. Educators watched students put skills they had learned in the classroom to use before the school community. This was an ideal opportunity to assess what students had learned.

Planning for Deliberation

Deliberation comes naturally to some students. They may be interested in current events, or they may possess skills that support interdependent learning. These students are typically eager to jump into deliberative units and often feel empowered when their teachers ask them to discuss controversial topics. The teacher can support these learners by providing specific feedback to focus their deliberations and class assignments in a way that promotes meaningful connections to academic standards.

Other students may struggle to fully participate in deliberative units. This may be due to their comfort level in dealing with conflicting ideas, a mismatch between their strengths and the communication skills used in deliberation, their academic skill set, or other issues. For example, teachers who use NIF in the classroom often report that middle school students and struggling readers have difficulty comprehending some NIF issue guides. These students may be overwhelmed by the complexity of the texts and vocabulary, or they may be unsure of how to approach nonfiction texts. On the other hand, teachers have shared that some of their most advanced learners, including gifted and honors students, have experienced frustration during deliberation units. Some of these students are accustomed to seeking the "one correct answer" or the "best answer," and may be less skilled at dealing with uncertainty or honoring the views and experiences of other learners.

In order to strengthen student participation in deliberation and the class activities associated with deliberative units, "educators need to use the same skills and strategies they use to differentiate instruction[53] in their other classes," says Joe Leavy. At Huntington High School, this means teachers take time to plan activities that ensure all students have access to a broad base of information about the issue and understand what is expected of them during a forum. To make sure social studies teachers are able to meet students' needs, special education teachers, teachers of the gifted, and ELL specialists may participate in professional development on deliberation so they are prepared to consult with teachers who are planning deliberative units or serve as coteachers or discussion moderators.

Nicole Mulholland, a certified special education teacher, partners with social studies teachers to coteach the required Participation in Government class for Huntington seniors. When I visited a classroom, I observed a group of students—which included individuals with learning disabilities and language differences—deliberating on America's role in the world. Because of the care that had been taken to prepare students for the forum, I could not distinguish the students who had problems reading the issue book from those who had breezed through the materials. All of the students offered informed opinions, referenced texts, and linked their ideas with those of their classmates. Mulholland and her coteacher carefully facilitated the discussion, posing questions to the group and probing answers to encourage students to consider trade-offs within each choice.

After the class, I asked the teachers what they had done to prepare the students for deliberation. I posed the same question to other teachers in the NIF network. They described a wide range of teaching strategies and assignments used to ensure that students were able to access key information to support participation in deliberative forums. In secondary classrooms, the most common strategies used were jigsaw activities, issue deconstruction assignments, NIF starter videos, and supplemental research on the issue. In elementary classrooms, teachers used reading-comprehension strategies like partner reading, annotation, and summarization. (Descriptions of some of these activities and assignments are included in the Appendices). Teachers also reported benefiting from additional staff support during their first few full-class forums. This was especially important for classes serving younger students, those with large enrollments (more than 25), and classes that included many students with language or reading difficulties.

As one teacher put it, "If we are serious about making sure all citizens feel like they have a seat at the table, we need to make sure we have 'set the stage' for students to participate as citizens in school." This includes supporting teacher learning and differentiating instruction[54] to ensure that diverse learners are fully included in classroom deliberations.

From Classroom Engagement to Civic Engagement

Deliberation can be a powerful strategy for engaging students in learning about issues, but it is especially effective in linking students to their roles as citizens. According to teachers in the NIF network, issue study and deliberation can address some fundamental needs that exist within democracy that take root, for some students, during their school years. "There is an apathy that exists about America's democracy that is in some measure due to a lack of understanding of the issues that face us," one teacher said. Another noted that, "schools tend to teach students to make choices behaviorally, but they do not teach students to make choices in an academic or political way." As a result, it is not surprising that many citizens limit their democratic participation to voting.

"If we are serious about making sure all citizens feel they have a seat at the table, we need to 'set the stage' for students to participate as citizens."

It is encouraging that students respond so favorably to classroom deliberation. However, teaching with deliberation carries with it some responsibilities. Educators who wish to leave no citizen-child behind should understand the goals of deliberation, make efforts to bring all students into political conversations, and support students who wish to apply deliberative decision making in their lives as citizens. The next chapter describes how teachers foster student voice and civic learning in Birmingham, Alabama, a community with a deep and proud history of civic engagement.

CHAPTER FOUR

Mentoring Citizens

The magic that happens inside a good teacher's classroom is hard to put a finger on because it is not episodic. Good teachers have usually honed their craft over time and developed approaches to teaching and learning that are well suited to their students and their context. They understand that teaching does not happen in a vacuum; both the teachers and their students have histories and experiences that affect their learning and orientation toward subject matter and authority. They also recognize that teachers have biases that can influence their work. The best teachers take these considerations into account. They try to improve their practice, build relationships with students and other teachers, and look beyond the standard curriculum for opportunities to teach important lessons.

Jessica Wedgeworth is one of those teachers. She teaches middle school social studies in the Birmingham City Schools. A lifelong resident of Birmingham, Wedgeworth understands the mind-sets of people in her community and the ways in which history and social conditions affect how children see themselves as learners. Despite desegregation, 95 percent of the students in the school district are black.[55]

Wedgeworth understands what this means for her community and its students. Regardless of their merits, they still live a world marked by racial divisions—where black citizens are less likely to experience economic mobility than their white counterparts,[56] and black youth are less likely to graduate from high school.[57] For Wedgeworth, racism is a reality that her students must recognize and confront; it should not limit them. That is why she believes part of her job is to mentor students—to help them make sense of the past and present and learn skills that will help them claim their own future.

Wedgeworth grew up in a tight-knit family and community, with aunts who were teachers and neighbors and family members who were engineers, doctors, and lawyers. She says there were many people in her life who worked hard and had a commitment to young people. Many had college degrees and professional jobs, but others were laborers or stay-at-home mothers who were connected by their commitment to raising and nurturing young people. They also had a strong work ethic. People like Wedgeworth's grandfather, a farmer, instilled in her the belief that citizens are "productive, self-sufficient, own property, and take care of the youth."

Wedgeworth was a successful student in high school and could envision many career options when she set off for college at the University of Alabama at Birmingham. At first, she aspired to work in business and pursued a major in computer science. She enjoyed the challenge of learning a new language and the excitement of venturing into a field that was unknown. But after only a few semesters, Wedgeworth realized something was missing. Computer science offered the promise of a job with good pay, but Wedgeworth could not see herself making a career of it. It just did not speak to her values. She needed a career that would allow her to emulate the people who made a difference in her own life. She wanted a job that allowed her to be an example to young people and to be of service to her community. Wedgeworth explains her motivation to teach in this way: "When I was young, there were a lot of people in the African American community who were mentors to me. People in my community were involved in young people's lives, and that made a huge difference. I decided to be a social studies teacher because it was a way to mentor youth and help them see all that is possible."

The power of mentorship is a prevailing storyline in Jessica Wedgeworth's life and career, just as it is in the lives of so many students. Yet too many accounts of the value of mentorship emphasize its importance only to youth who are disadvantaged in some way—youth who are often referred to as at-risk. Wedgeworth was not a disadvantaged child. She was raised in a middle-class community, in a family that valued education and gave her lots of love. Her mentors were successful people in her community who spent time with her, got to know her, and encouraged her to try new things. She learned from her mentors how to be an active citizen.

When Wedgeworth finally made the decision to become a teacher, there was little question in her mind about the grade level she would teach. She said it had to be middle school because, "that is when kids really start to need mentors the most." During the middle-school years, young people begin to seek independence from their parents. It is a time when they begin to feel self-conscious and become susceptible to the influence of peers. It is also a time when youth, who still have deep roots at home, begin to venture out and exert influence on their world. Working as a social studies teacher in a middle school allows Wedgeworth to teach important lessons about history, but it also allows her to "teach students how to be citizens with agency," she stated. "It is important for them to understand the system and know how to work to make the community a better place."

Jessica Wedgeworth began her career as an eighth-grade world-history teacher in a neighborhood school in Birmingham. After five years in that school, Wedgeworth applied for and received a transfer to the John Herbert Phillips Academy, a selective International Baccalaureate K-8 school in the heart of downtown Birmingham. The move was prompted by her daughter's experience at Phillips Academy and Wedgeworth's interest in working in a school that had a clear mission and strong parental support. As a parent, Wedgeworth liked the fact that the school emphasized close teacher-parent collaboration. She also liked the fact that the school was still in its infancy, having been established only a year before. There were many opportunities for committed teachers to make their mark on the school and influence how the institution supported students. "It was a huge leap of faith," Wedgeworth said. "But it was worth it."

In her first year of working at Phillips Academy, she played an active role in the parent-teacher organization and became involved in numerous extracurricular programs. Wedgeworth was first introduced to deliberation in the classroom when she attended a professional-development workshop in the summer following her first year at Phillips Academy. Jackie Jackson, a curriculum specialist in the school district, and Peggy Sparks, then assistant to the superintendent of the Birmingham City Schools, led the workshop. Sparks is a local civil-rights leader, community organizer, and indefatigable advocate for youth. As Sparks talked to the teachers about the importance of citizens who deliberate, Wedgeworth thought about her passion for mentoring young citizens and how useful the skills of deliberation could be for her students. She immediately recognized that deliberation offered something more than other approaches to teaching citizenship. It could teach students how to deal with big and complicated problems, while giving them tools to understand and work with people who have a different view of how things should be.

Reframing Curricula

Inspired by Peggy Sparks's passion, and with the support of Jackie Jackson and other teacher leaders, Wedgeworth and a cadre of Birmingham social studies teachers began experimenting with deliberation in the classroom in 2009. While the teachers' initial work with deliberation involved classroom forums supported by NIF issue guides, the practice of deliberation in the classroom evolved over the years, taking on different looks from one school to the next, and from one classroom to the next within the same school. Wedgeworth, for example, still uses NIF guides and forums to address themes in her World Cultures class; however, her students are now more involved in leading classroom forums and planning civic action. When there is no NIF issue guide that connects to a theme in the curriculum, Wedgeworth reframes topics in her curriculum to promote deeper, more deliberative classroom conversations.

Reframing the curriculum refers to an intentional decision by the teacher to present content in a way that fosters deliberation.

"Reframing the curriculum" is a term used by many educators who teach deliberation in the classroom. In general, reframing refers to an intentional decision by the teacher to present curricular content in a way that fosters deliberation by increasing students' exposure to diverse perspectives, choices, and trade-offs that are inherent within topics of study. It also refers to two related terms associated with NIF-style forums—naming and framing:

- *Naming* refers to the way a problem or topic is identified or introduced to students (or citizens). The name given to a problem influences how it is discussed, as well as the range of ideas and options that are considered.[58] Often the way a problem is named leads people to a particular understanding or response. By naming issues in ways that do not suggest a single answer, teachers can build rich and engaging units of study that highlight choices inherent within historic decisions or contemporary issues, including what was or is at stake for different stakeholders. Table 4a demonstrates how the issue of immigration might be named to reflect different ways of understanding the issue.

- *Framing* refers to the options or perspectives used to understand an issue or problem, as well as critical information, drawbacks, and trade-offs associated with different approaches.[59] A well-designed deliberative framework highlights three or four broad perspectives that will be explored in a deliberative unit. *Prescriptive framings* direct students or citizens to a predetermined or preferred outcome, and may limit the range of options or perspectives considered. In other words, the quality of the deliberation is influenced by the quality of the framing.

Table 4a: Naming an Issue (Example: How should the US approach immigration?)

Immigration is a/an:	Some possible framings and trade-offs
safety and security issue	Immigration is a security issue that can increase the likelihood that a dangerous person will enter the US. Safety should be the first priority in any approach to immigration, even if that means refugees suffer and American companies are less competitive.
economic competitiveness / innovation issue	America is lacking human resources to fill many low-skill and high-skill jobs and this can inhibit growth, innovation, and adaptation in the new economy. Immigration policies should be flexible, efficient, and responsive to market needs, even if that means some people will have easier entry into America than others.
cultural/community development issue	Immigrants can contribute to the nation and community in important ways: through their contributions to the arts, as tax payers, and as neighbors. The focus of immigration policies should be bridging divides between immigrants and Americans to foster thriving, diverse communities, even if it means less tax funding is available for screening efforts and special visa programs.

When Wedgeworth and other teachers reframe their curriculum to promote deliberation, they look for a broad theme and then develop an open-ended question based on the theme that, if answered, would require both citizen action and policy action. The theme, named as a question, establishes an inquiry orientation to the unit that can focus students' reading, study, and research. Table 4b provides some sample inquiry questions used by teachers in the NIF Teachers Network. Some of these questions connect directly to NIF issue guides; others do not.

Table 4b: Sample Inquiry Questions

Unit/Subject	Deliberative Inquiry Questions
American History	How should the colonies respond to concerns about British taxation and rule?
Environmentalism, climate, and ecology	What is the best approach for dealing with climate issues in 2016?
Industrialization, 20th century migration, globalization	How are immigration policies era-specific, and what three or four approaches might the US consider today?

As these questions suggest, there is not a single approach to reframing topics in curricula. However, there are some common elements teachers might consider when developing deliberative curriculum frameworks for use in schools. The frameworks typically include:

- key information and vocabulary the teacher would like their students to learn;

- three to four choices or options for responding to the issue. These should be understandable, and should align with how everyday people may talk about the issue. Ideally, the approaches would not align with partisan framings or the views of specific actors or groups, although the framework should offer a way to explore the values and concerns of major as well as marginalized perspectives;

- key information, sample policy actions, and some information about the strengths and limitations of each option, as well as trade-offs;

- links to primary and secondary sources that represent different perspectives on the themes.

The framing process, when done as a traditional curriculum-planning exercise, is typically an iterative process that involves adapting the original inquiry question as new information and resources become available. In its final form, the deliberative unit may involve students in studying each of the three options in preparation for small-group deliberation or a classroom forum. During forums, students examine each option and answer questions designed to engage them in weighing or deciding on actions. Questions might include:

- What are the key ideas and strategic facts associated with the option?

- What are the benefits of this option? What do you like about this option? What is most valuable to people who agree with this approach?

- What concerns you about this option? What are the drawbacks?

- If citizens embraced this option, what would they need to give up? (What are the trade-offs?)

- (After all options have been discussed) What should we do? What common ground did we identify?

These types of questions promote comprehension (question 1) and more. By asking students to state the best case for each option and the legitimate values held by those who favor it (question 2), students develop an understanding of perspectives that do not align with their own. When asked to consider the concerns or drawbacks of each option (question 3), students are engaged in critique of perspectives that may seem reasonable to them at face value. Finally, questions that address trade-offs (question 4), reinforce the reality that there are no perfect solutions to public issues, but some options may be more viable than others at a particular point in time.

According to Wedgeworth, "these are important ideas and lessons," particularly for teachers who want to instill agency in their students. "Even though my students live in communities where issues are so prevalent in their lives, we have not always taught about social issues in a way that helps them to think about others' perspectives and what can realistically be done."

From Talk to Action

Educators in the NIF Teachers Network recognize the intrinsic value of teaching students how to think and talk deliberatively. They also recognize the value of teaching deliberation as an approach to group decision making. Yet public deliberation, at its core, is about engaging citizens in public life in a way that helps them connect to issues and to their fellow citizens; it helps them recognize new opportunities for taking action to make their communities stronger. While there are benefits to citizens talking deliberatively, society benefits most directly when citizens are able to translate deliberative talk into civic action.

Wedgeworth concedes that it is not always easy to provide opportunities for students to act as citizens in the school. "Middle schoolers can see the connection between issues and actions. The challenge is finding the time and focusing students' energy so they can follow through on their passions." She admits that sometimes the best she can do is encourage students to act on their concerns outside of the classroom.

This is exactly what Wedgeworth did for Alexandra, a student at Phillips Academy. After participating in a deliberative unit in Wedgeworth's class, Alexandra wanted to do something to stem the drop-out problem in her community. The unit required students to examine the educational system in different counties, consider factors that placed students at risk of limited education in these contexts, and propose solutions. Through her research, Alexandra discovered that many American students who drop out of school begin losing interest in formal education as early as third or fourth grade. This concerned her. Because Phillips Academy is a K-8 school, Alexandra felt compelled to initiate a drop-out prevention project that targeted third and fourth graders in her school.

When Alexandra came to Wedgeworth with her idea, Wedgeworth knew it was something the school could support, but, as an already over-scheduled teacher, she could not dedicate the time needed to supervise the project. Instead, she listened to Alexandra's ideas and helped her develop a realistic plan. Wedgeworth then worked behind the scenes to ensure her principal and fellow teachers knew Alexandra might be seeking their support. Confident that her colleagues understood the context of Alexandra's request, Wedgeworth stepped back and let Alexandra work within the structure of the school to advocate for and implement her plan. Within two weeks, Alexandra had met with the principal, presented her idea to the third and fourth grade teachers, and was well on her way to starting a tutoring and mentoring program linking eighth-graders and elementary students. That year, Alexandra and two other eighth-graders mentored several students two to three days per week in the school's multi-purpose learning center.

"Teaching facts is one of the least important things I do. Helping students learn to think critically and interact across groups is much more important."

- JohnMark Edwards

Wedgeworth is quick to note that most students at Phillips Academy are not prepared to do what Alexandra did when they enter sixth grade. As an eighth-grader, Alexandra's actions were supported by capacities nurtured by teachers' efforts to use and promote active forms of civic learning. At Phillips, civic learning is explicitly addressed in social studies classrooms and through the school's extracurricular offerings, which range from competitive sports to special-interest clubs to planned and ad-hoc service-learning projects that respond to real community needs. Teachers play formal and informal roles in supporting civic learning, guided by a shared vision that Phillips is preparing students to be global leaders.

Real Practice

On the day I visited Phillips Academy, I spent time in two different classrooms: Jessica Wedgeworth's fifth-period class and a seventh-grade class taught by JohnMark Edwards. Like other classes I had visited, I noticed that the two teachers had distinct styles and orientations, which influenced the tone of their classes and students' interactions with one another.

Wedgeworth's class was more traditional, with students at desks and walls covered with carefully designed bulletin boards showcasing student work and class themes. Edwards's class was informal and bustling with activity. Rather than sitting at desks, the class was arranged so that students sat in clusters at tables or on couches that had been placed strategically around the room. The walls were covered with maps, artifacts from around the world, *Time* magazine covers, and posters created by students to represent their learning.

The items displayed on Edwards's walls were chosen intentionally to convey the idea that social studies and history are more than abstract ideas or past events— that they truly influence who we are and who we are becoming as individuals and as a society. "History is not just a timeline of events," said Edwards. "It is something we are creating and recreating all the time."

Like Wedgeworth, JohnMark Edwards plays a key role in knitting together Phillips Academy's civic-learning program through his active involvement in shaping the school's curriculum and after-school programs. Edwards believes deliberation adds value to the formal curriculum and helps link together many seemingly disparate learning experiences. "Teaching facts in a social studies class is one of the least important things I do. Helping students learn to think critically, work through differences, and interact across groups is much more important."

JohnMark Edwards is a notable figure at Phillips Academy. On the surface, he stands out as one of the few Caucasian adults in the school. When you look deeper and spend time talking with him, you find that he has a very unique perspective on the purposes of education, informed by a childhood spent attending Embassy schools, a language academy, a progressive Costa Rican private school, and a suburban Chicago high school. Through those experiences, Edwards developed a deep appreciation of different cultures and a critical awareness of what is missing from most Americans' school experiences:

> Most American kids do not have the opportunity to get to know people who are vastly different from them, much less work with those people to achieve a common good. My passion is building bridges across communities, across people groups . . . to make sure more kids have the opportunity to experience difference, challenge stereotypes, and develop relationships with people they would have never known.

In addition to his teaching responsibilities, Edwards is coach of the Phillips Academy lacrosse team and a co-advisor to the Junior Model United Nations club. Both of these activities bring his students in close contact with students from suburban schools. These suburban youth, who are mostly white, may come to the competition with preconceived ideas about what Birmingham students are like. "They may expect less of my students because of what they have been told about black people or what they have seen in the media," explained Edwards. "After they meet my students and have competed with them, they have a different impression."

The concept of "deliberative citizens" permeates Edwards's work with students. "Whenever I work with students, I begin by highlighting and reinforcing deliberative skills. This is how we conduct ourselves. We think hard, ask questions, and deliberate through our problems. Whether it is a small or large issue we are facing, deliberation is how we conduct ourselves."

To help students learn how to keep problem-solving conversations productive, he provides ground rules for the conversations early in the year. Students are expected to listen to each other and respond in one of three ways:

- Agree with the person who just spoke and explain why you agree;

- Respectfully disagree and give a reason for disagreeing;

- Add something to the conversation by building on what has been said.

Over time, students begin to adopt this communication heuristic and, eventually, begin to combine response options and deviate from it. For example, a student may respectfully disagree with part of what a classmate says and then add to the part of the idea with which he agrees.

Edwards believes that it is important for students to have real-life opportunities to use deliberative communication and problem-solving skills. That is why he provides opportunities for his students to self-organize around issues with minimal teacher intervention. "I might ask my team or class to plan a service project to commemorate International Women's Day or Earth Day," he stated. "Then I divide them into small groups to develop proposals [for consideration by their peers]."

When the groups present their proposal to the class (or team), Edwards encourages them to deliberate about the merits and trade-offs of each proposal, using questions that promote deliberation. Once the group agrees on a project concept, they begin planning the event with additional teacher support. Throughout the process, Edwards reinforces deliberative communication skills and questioning.

For Edwards, the essence of his work with students is about preparing each of them to be a citizen who feels comfortable talking about any public issue, and who has the skills to engage in deliberative problem solving and take civic action. While it can be challenging to teach students how to work across racial divides within a segregated school, JohnMark Edwards and Jessica Wedgeworth have found that the skills of deliberation are generalizable to contexts outside of the classroom. This is especially true if students are given opportunities to apply what they have learned in settings where they interact with students from other communities.

Mentoring Citizens

Many first-hand accounts of successful citizens' lives describe the positive influence of an adult mentor in their development. Indeed, natural mentors, like teachers, coaches, and youth leaders can play an important role in providing support to students who are experiencing challenges in their personal lives. Mentors can play a role in supporting the development of interests and capacities in students that may not be nurtured in the home.[60] Finally, as this chapter demonstrates, mentors can play a role in broadening students' conceptions of public issues and citizenship. Teachers who use deliberation can help students see an alternative to the forms of citizenship elevated by the media, and can equip students to connect deliberation to civic action.

While there is scant research on this type of civic mentorship, the concept emerged as a strong theme in my interviews with teachers who use deliberation in the classroom. Across schools, teachers noted the value of introducing another way of thinking, talking, and problem solving to students, as well as promoting a form of politics that can bring marginalized voices into decision making. Some teachers concerned with elevating marginalized voices tended to focus on preparing students for civil, but critical, conversations. Others chose to emphasize the perspectives of marginalized groups by asking students to consider "whose voice is not in the room." In Birmingham, the issue of voice is complex, and is influenced by the racial divisions that are still prevalent in the community.

By providing many different experiences that involve deliberation, students become more comfortable framing and expressing their ideas.

According to one Birmingham school administrator, "Many (Southern) African American families have taught their children not to talk in public. 'Don't express honest ideas because it will get you in trouble.' . . . Under Jim Crow Alabama, and even in the years since, things could turn bad quickly for black people who spoke up." As a result, "We locked our children down" by not letting them out of the house and by not letting them talk about anything political. "Those cultural taboos linger, even today," she said. Birmingham teachers who use deliberation in the classroom "don't allow students to be invisible like they may want to be, like they may have been taught to be. We address the reticence they have and we teach them to draw attention to themselves and their ideas."

Deliberation is one of the strategies Birmingham teachers use to support civic learning. By providing many different experiences that involve deliberation, students become more comfortable framing and expressing their ideas in different ways, and they become more critical consumers of media on public issues. From there, teachers can connect the practice to other forms of civic learning, discourse, and action, including those associated with procedural democracy, community organizing, and protest.

CHAPTER FIVE

Historic Decisions and Citizens' Work

Donnan Stoicovy was a school principal for almost 28 years, but you will never hear her use that word. She refers to herself as the "lead learner" of Park Forest Elementary School, a K-5 school in State College, Pennsylvania. Like many educators, Stoicovy recognizes that learning is a lifelong process; however, her perspective on school leadership goes beyond a commitment to continuous learning. After 41 years of work in education, Stoicovy sees public school leadership as a democratic enterprise. School improvement is not something leaders facilitate from the top. It requires teachers, parents, and students to share in the school's governance through the posing of problems, inquiry, and action. The outcome of effective school leadership, according to Stoicovy, is a community that can identify and solve problems that impact student development and learning.

Stoicovy and the teachers at Park Forest Elementary model this vision of success. There, everyone is encouraged to discuss issues that affect their classes, school, and community at large. During regular meetings at both the classroom and school-wide level, students discuss problems, ask questions, share research, and propose strategies to make their communities better. Students and teachers then work together to implement students' strategies, and eventually come back together to reflect on and refine their responses based upon what they have learned.

Stoicovy can provide many examples of how this type of learning has enhanced the school. Yet she is most proud of the way the school's commitment to dialogue and inquiry has influenced how children see themselves as citizens and problem solvers beyond the classroom—sometimes, for problems that emerge thousands of miles away.

An example of this occurred in 2010, when Haiti suffered a devastating earthquake that killed over 160,000 people and left hundreds of thousands without homes, food, or basic sanitation. As students entered the school a day after the disaster, Stoicovy noticed a somber tone among the children. She didn't initially recognize it as a reaction to the earthquake since the media coverage had hardly begun and the extent of the devastation was still unclear. Yet as students passed in the hallway, teachers began to pick up on their quiet conversations. Over and over, they heard a common sentiment uttered by the children: "We need to help. But what should we do?"

Beginning in kindergarten, Park Forest students talk about how their choices affect others and what it means to be a part of a community.

In the hours and weeks that followed, Park Forest students focused their efforts on answering the inquiry question, "What is the best way for us to help the Haitian people?" With the support of their teachers, students began by researching the needs and the potential impact of different humanitarian responses. Students learned that first responders were meeting most of the immediate needs of Haitians, so they focused on meeting long-term needs. From there, classes continued their research and developed proposals for how to help. The proposals were discussed at class-level and school-wide meetings, where they were critiqued and refined. Eventually, the school community chose to support a charity several classes had researched: Houses for Haiti. Students then organized fundraising efforts that were launched in grade-level and after-school meetings.

"Students were empowered to take ownership of the problem and they did. That's what most impressed me," said Stoicovy. "Although the teachers served as guides, the effort was fueled by the students' drive to make a difference." By the end of the year, Park Forest students had raised and donated over $2,000 to Houses for Haiti. More important, students had an authentic experience of active citizenship.

Park Forest Elementary is not the only elementary school in the United States that engages students in responding to local and international needs. Indeed, survey research suggests that school-recognized and school-supported community service is common in elementary schools across the United States, with approximately 50 percent of schools emphasizing service in some form.[61] Through participation in community service, students learn important interpersonal and civic skills while applying academic learning to real-world situations.[62] Students are empowered to identify problems, conduct research, and pose solutions as part of the process of mobilizing for civic action. This process, known as service learning, takes time to organize and it can be fraught with the challenges and frustrations of active citizenship.[63]

At Park Forest Elementary, students have many different opportunities to engage in service and practice citizenship at school, including school-wide service-learning projects, classroom council meetings, and peer-helper programs. Through such hands-on experiences, students learn that being an active citizen involves more than voting. It involves doing the types of things citizens do to improve their community, including talking and acting to address community problems and participating in community decision making.

Beginning in kindergarten, Park Forest students talk about how their choices affect others and what it means to be a part of a community. As they move up the grades, students provide more and more input into decisions that affect their classrooms and school. For example, each year, Park Forest students help to set their own classroom rules, and classes take turns facilitating weekly whole-school meetings known as "community meetings." At community meetings, students go through an agenda where they provide updates on current events and address topics relevant to students and the school. In the past, students have used these meetings to plan efforts to achieve a "zero waste" school and solicit input on the Park Forest "Bill of Rights." Younger students' contributions to community meetings are valued and encouraged, while older students model complex civic skills and behaviors.

Developing Historical Thinkers

Public deliberation, as it is defined within these pages, is part of the fifth-grade experience at Park Forest. It is built into the US history curriculum through an approach known as "Historic Decisions," a term coined by NIF and the educators described in this book. It refers to the practice of reframing historical moments in a way that highlights the choices faced by citizens and leaders. Currently, there are two official NIF Historic Decisions guides, a free series developed by the National Archives on presidential decisions, and several other forthcoming issue guides framed by other institutions (for a list of current resources, see Appendix E). Classroom and university teachers, as well as museum educators, are using these guides and the deliberative process to encourage historical thinking and linkages between history learning and civic learning.

Park Forest teacher Lori McGarry uses Historic Decisions issue guides as part of a unit on early America, during which her students study and engage in simulations of colonial life. They deliberate about the concerns facing the colonies and its citizens at the time of independence and in the days leading up to the Constitutional Convention using the NIF issue guides *1776: What Should We Do?* and *A New Land: What Kind of Government Should We Have?* Both resources present three approaches that could have been taken by early Americans to solve problems of governance. Rather than presenting independence and the United States as inevitable outcomes, the resources provide a range of different options that could have informed early Americans' decisions.

Teachers like McGarry tell the story of America and its important moments by engaging students with the concerns of early Americans. Students learn about issues faced by citizens and leaders, consider choices that could have been made, discuss trade-offs that might have resulted, and reflect on the role of citizens in the decision-making process. This approach provides a concrete way for students to connect themes in history to current events, as well as to their own lives, according to McGarry. After the deliberation on 1776, McGarry's students discussed the significance of the decision to declare independence from Britain. Without much prompting from their teacher, students noted how risky declaring independence was, the courage exhibited by everyday Americans who joined the fight, and the unusual solidarity that occurred within diverse colonies. Students were also able to articulate why some Virginians and Bostonians may have joined the war effort for different reasons. And they understood why some colonists might have favored a more moderate option, such as negotiating a new governance arrangement with Britain.

The type of learning students experience in McGarry's class helps them master historical timelines and key facts because she weaves deliberation into larger units of study that present information sequentially, engage students with primary source documents, and allow students to experience colonial life. But deliberation offers something more than historical simulations, according to Donnan Stoicovy. Deliberation about historical issues helps connect what students are learning in history to the school's broader civic-learning agenda. It also reinforces understanding of the plight and perspectives of citizens living in different times and different places, something known as historical perspective-taking, or historical empathy.[64] Through public deliberation on historic decisions, students learn about choices that defined history and develop skills for making choices in their own lives. When reflecting on the learning process, McGarry's students reported that deliberation taught them: "how to speak with others about problems, realizing that every side of a problem has some pros and cons"; "that it is important to hear other people's sides and not just the side that you are on"; and "how to look at a problem from multiple perspectives . . . before you make a choice."

Deliberation about historical issues helps connect what students are learning in history to the school's broader civic-learning agenda.

Deliberation about historic decisions disposes students to look beyond a single narrative of history to find other ways of understanding and interpreting historical events based upon evidence. This approach does not minimize the popular narrative, but broadens students' awareness of alternative perspectives and citizens' roles in democracy at key points in history.

From History to Framing Students' Concerns

In the spring of 2015, Lori McGarry decided to take her work with Historic Decisions one step further. After engaging her class in forums on *1776* and *A New Land*, McGarry wanted to make the connection between deliberation and citizenship more explicit. She knew her students were up for a challenge. They had experienced a five-year immersive elementary program emphasizing community, citizenship, and service learning. She knew most of her students cared about the school and believed they had a responsibility to make choices that made a difference. She was also familiar with the deliberative work of classrooms in Alabama, Wisconsin, and New York. There, middle and high school students learned to frame their own issues for deliberation and moderate deliberative forums in their communities. McGarry suspected her class could do this as well, if she provided the right type of support and scaffolding.

After consultation with teachers who had done similar work, McGarry decided to experiment with the naming and framing process. During a class in late April, she asked her students to brainstorm about issues that affected the school community. She asked them to consider topics that prevented the school from "being its best" and concerns that were not usually talked about. The students came up with a list of eight different topics. McGarry then asked them to narrow the list to one or two common concerns. Through a discussion and a nominating process, one of the issues rose to the top of the students' list: recess on gym days. This was a long-standing controversial issue in the school community. On physical education (PE) days, Park Forest students were not provided a recess period because, they were told, PE served the same purpose as recess, providing time for movement and exercise.

Most Park Forest fifth-graders disagreed with this rationale (that is, the naming of the issue). During follow-up class discussions of the issue, students were passionate in stating that recess was an opportunity to "see our friends from other classes," "get our energy out," "play what we want to play," or "just chill." These activities were important, they argued, because fifth-graders are still learning important social skills and how to be independent. To them, recess was more than a time for structured exercise. It was time for socializing, free play, relaxation, and deciding for oneself how to spend free time. Like adult citizens who often feel disconnected from experts' naming of public issues, McGarry's fifth-graders rejected the way school leaders had named the PE-recess issue because it did not speak to the things they held valuable. Yet like many citizens, they had little experience bridging their concerns with the concerns of authorities.

The issue-framing process offered a way for student-citizens to look at the recess problem from different points of view and consider other approaches to the problem. McGarry's issue-framing unit was conducted intermittently over a month-long period, between other curricular activities. She had students start by researching the benefits of recess, popular arguments in favor of and against it, and relevant policies. She then tasked them with writing persuasive essays on the topic—an assignment that involved skills that would be tested on Pennsylvania's state exams. Once completed, the essays were submitted to Donnan Stoicovy for her consideration.

After reviewing the students' essays, Stoicovy visited the class to provide additional background information on her role, state mandates regarding instructional minutes, and the origin of the district policy. She explained that the PE-recess policy applied to all elementary schools in the district and had been initiated in response to state requirements regarding instructional minutes. Students asked clarifying questions of Stoicovy and, together, they discussed underlying concerns of students and adults. Once Stoicovy and McGarry were satisfied that the students had sufficient background information, they divided the class into small groups and asked each to develop a list of actions that could be taken and concerns to be addressed. Students were then asked to propose three different approaches to addressing the PE-recess problem.

Stoicovy and McGarry did not directly facilitate any of the student groups; however, they asked students to assume specific roles (such as group facilitator, recorder, fact-checker) and reminded them of the ground rules for group work. This empowered each student to take ownership of the issue and the framing process, while a clear structure of tasks, roles, and ground rules helped to ensure the group process was productive.

When I visited Park Forest Elementary and McGarry's class several weeks after their initial issue-framing activity, they had coalesced around three options for restoring recess on PE days. For each of the options, students in small groups were in the process of identifying benefits and trade-offs. The options included:

- Option 1: Shorten recess by 5-6 minutes on non-PE days to 20-24-minute recess each day;

- Option 2: Lobby the school board to change the school schedule, providing a slightly longer school day with extra time allotted to recess;

- Option 3: Petition the state department of education, asking them to reduce the required number of instructional hours each year from 900 to 882. This would allow an additional 30 minutes per week to be allotted for recess within the regular school schedule.

From the children's small-group conversations, it became clear that the students in McGarry's class had learned that the PE-recess issue was much more complicated than they had originally thought. They had also come to understand that their principal had limited power to change a district policy, and that state mandates often required school districts to make trade-offs. They concluded that any effort to change the policy would need to involve work with decision makers, and may need to target folks outside of the school. The options the students identified focused on three different levels of civic action that would target school-level decision-making processes (Option 1), district-level decision-making processes

(Option 2), and state-level decision-making processes (Option 3). Although it was a prescriptive framing, and did not engage students in exploring larger questions of school organization and curricula, McGarry's students had successfully applied the skills of naming, framing, and deliberation to their own civic organizing—an impressive feat.[65]

As I watched the students work in groups, McGarry shared her impressions of what they had learned. "Deliberation has been an incredible process for this class," she said. "I have seen a lot of growth in these students. As a group, they tended to be impulsive, immature, and bit self-absorbed—like many groups of fifth-graders. The deliberative process helped them to get outside of themselves. I now hear them say things like 'that wouldn't work because of this or that trade-off,' rather than just expecting to get their way because they think it's a good idea."

After sharing her overall impressions of how deliberation had changed her class, McGarry suggested that the impact on individual students might be even more profound. She called my attention to Timothy, a student who was known for always having the "right" answer. Like many citizens, McGarry said, he had a tendency to "get frustrated with people who took a longer time getting to his place, or when people shared a different point of view." While deliberating *1776*, he approached the teacher and expressed dissatisfaction with the deliberative process. "I don't understand why we are doing this if we can just read about the answer. It's wasting a lot of time."

"In democracy, we sometimes work on solving problems that are big and messy. We participate in processes that may seem frustrating. We do it because we are trying to get to a better place as a society."

- Lori McGarry

McGarry took his question as an opportunity to explain why the teachers at Park Forest spend so much time engaging students in this type of work. "In community life, in democracy, we sometimes work on solving problems that are big and messy. We work on solving problems that may not directly affect us, but they matter for other people. We participate in processes that may seem frustrating or that take a long time. But we keep working. We do it because we are trying to get to a better place as a society."

She then suggested that I keep an eye on Timothy. Like students in the other groups, he was working to flesh out the trade-offs associated with one of the PE-recess options. I watched the young boy, with brown shaggy hair, sitting on the ground with his peers, marker in hand. He asked his classmates questions, listened to their responses, and wrote their ideas, along with his, on the poster board. There were no brilliant statements or fireworks. Just a young boy and his peers trying to make sense of something together, trying to create a tool that could help them make a better decision.

"You see," said McGarry, "he's with his group. He's part of the community. He's sticking to this process and he is contributing. . . . He may still think the process is inefficient (or he has the best answer), but he is willing to stay engaged as a citizen of this class. . . . It may sound crazy, but this is one little approximation of democracy in school."

Deliberation and Historic Decisions in High School

Teaching with deliberation is not just confined to Park Forest Elementary in State College. The State College Area High School (SCAHS) has been using deliberation in the classroom since the late 1990s. At that time, Dave Dillon, a high school social studies teacher, forged a partnership with a community group known as Public Issues Forums of Centre County (PIFCC) and some faculty members at Penn State University. Together, volunteers and teachers collaborated to introduce NIF issues to high school students, and experimented with ways of adapting public deliberation for use in social studies classrooms. Over time, the partnership became well known; more teachers adopted deliberative teaching methods, a current-issues course was proposed and approved by the school board, and students gained recognition for their role in framing issues and moderating community forums.

When Dave Dillon left State College to pursue a leadership opportunity in another school district, deliberation in the classroom was codified in the curriculum of the SCAHS public issues course. Today, the partnership with PIFCC remains, supported by a school board member involved in PIFCC and teachers, including Jon Lodge, who are involved in convening yearly teachers institutes in the area.

Like other teachers who have been working with deliberation for years, Lodge has adapted aspects of the deliberative process for use across the curriculum. While he still uses the occasional NIF issue guide, visitors to his classroom are more apt to see him:

- presenting three or four perspectives on a theme;

- asking students to identify the concerns of different historical actors and groups from primary source documents and secondary accounts;

- posing the question: "Whose voices are not represented in this text (or in our discussion)? What might they say?"

- asking students to find common ground among several different perspectives on an issue.

Even his daily questioning techniques are directed at promoting deliberation. When I visited his class, he was teaching about Gandhi's role in India's history and his movement's relationship with other nonviolent movements.

The students had been watching the feature film *Gandhi* for the last two days and had almost reached the point in the movie where the Amritsar Massacre takes place. Periodically, as students watched the film, Lodge stopped the video and called their attention to questions on their study guide. He asked them to state different characters' perspectives on key events in the film, and how that perspective related to what the character held valuable. Over the course of the movie, he expected students would be able to see how perspectives shifted as tensions in values emerged and action became necessary as the result of growing political unrest.

I watched as Lodge masterfully posed questions to promote students' critical thinking about history. Based upon their comments, it was clear Lodge's students were experiencing the same type of historical empathy that Lori McGarry's students felt during the *New Land* deliberation. For example, after observing the events at Amritsar, Lodge asked students to describe how the British military's actions may have influenced politically conservative and moderate Indians, as well as mainland British expatriates. Some predicted that concerns about personal security would reinforce feelings of nationalism. Others noted that moderates may have chosen to retreat from nationalist positions. A few wondered how Gandhi's commitments would change as he faced tensions between his value of a unified country and the threat the British Empire posed for vulnerable groups in India. As students grappled with this historic moment, Lodge asked them to name some of the options Gandhi had and the trade-offs each option presented.

It is the type of work that active citizens have engaged in throughout time, and it is often missing from the way history is taught in schools.

For Lodge and his students, a structured forum was not necessary to elicit deliberative thinking. What was important was the teacher's approach to the curriculum and the questions posed. For many teachers involved in this research, NIF has been an introduction to deliberative pedagogy. After using NIF guides or locally framed issue guides, teachers have gone on to adapt their curricula and teaching methods to provide opportunities for students to engage in deliberation.[66] It is the type of work that active citizens have engaged in throughout time, and it is often missing from the way history is taught in schools.

CHAPTER SIX

Teachers Institutes: More than Professional Development

Retired school administrator Peggy Sparks is a community leader and lifelong resident of Birmingham, Alabama. Teachers revere her because she is energetic, optimistic, and she gets things done. Her picture hangs in the grand entry of the Birmingham Civil Rights Institute, of which she was a founding board member. She has been a proponent of active citizenship in schools for as long as anyone can remember—longer, surely, than her 40-plus years of working in public schools. Her work with NIF and public deliberation is just one example of this. She has been hosting and moderating public forums in Birmingham for at least 30 years in her informal capacity as citizen and in her formal roles with the school district and other community institutions.

In 2008, Sparks laid the groundwork for the establishment of the Birmingham Teachers Institute,[67] a partnership involving the Birmingham City Schools, Miles College, and the David Mathews Center for Civic Life in Montevallo, Alabama. The institute hosts summer professional development workshops for teachers who are interested in using deliberation in the classroom. After teachers attend a workshop, Sparks and her son, Curtis, provide follow-up support. They stay in email communication with teachers, visit classrooms, model deliberative teaching strategies, and build support for teachers' work within the school district and community.

Sparks is not a professional development provider in the traditional sense. She is a partner, an advocate, and a model of deliberative citizenship. Sparks built support in the community for the Birmingham Teachers Institute by linking the work of teachers with a community advisory board that is active in convening deliberative forums in Birmingham. The individuals involved on the board have provided moral and material support to school-based deliberation efforts over the years. Some board members have visited classrooms to observe forums and recognize students' and teachers' efforts. Others have hosted recognition dinners for students who have shown leadership in linking classroom forums to community issues. Some have even provided financial support to the teachers institute. When people voiced concerns about whether teachers would be willing to drive to a teachers institute hosted at a historical site outside of Birmingham, a board member and business leader arranged for buses to transport them.

The type of support for deliberation that Peggy Sparks nurtures in the community lends credibility to the teachers' efforts. JohnMark Edwards and Jessica Wedgeworth, teachers at the John Herbert Phillips Academy, both noted that Sparks's advocacy and support have played an important role in rooting deliberation in their school. Because Sparks is a retired assistant to the superintendent of Birmingham City Schools, she understands how deliberation connects to other opportunities and needs in the district. When Birmingham City Schools applied for and received a federal Teaching American History grant in 2007, Sparks worked with curriculum leaders to link deliberation to the grant's broader goals. She also played an active role in helping to bring other partners to the table in support of the district's grant application.

Activities that connect people, aspirations, and democratic practices have been critical to the effort to sustain deliberation in the classroom.

The types of activities Sparks engages in—activities that connect people, aspirations, and democratic practices—have been critical to the effort to expand and sustain deliberation in the classroom in Birmingham. Indeed, since 2009, over 80 teachers have learned to use deliberation in the classroom through participation in a Birmingham Teachers Institute. The Birmingham City Schools' social studies department even adopted deliberation as one of its core pedagogical practices. Yet these strategic efforts might not have been as successful if Sparks's efforts were isolated from work at the classroom level. "You really need to understand what's happening in the classroom and what teachers need to make this work," Sparks says. "The teachers are the ones who are doing the heavy lifting and we need to support them where they are."

Making Space for Deliberation in Schools and Communities

Teachers who use deliberation in the classroom notice important differences in how their students think and engage in learning compared to students in classes that aren't exposed to deliberation. Students who learn to deliberate often demonstrate critical thinking skills, awareness of diverse perspectives, and the ability to synthesize information in ways that further individual and group learning. These are important civic skills, and they are associated with important classroom behaviors. In order to understand the strengths of a perspective that is not one's own, students must learn to listen deeply, ask probing questions, and draw connections between ideas. In order to decide together, groups of students must be able to balance personal interests with the interests of others while working to identify solutions based upon common principles. This process involves synthesis of the group's ideas, as well as consideration of perspectives not represented in the room.

Teaching for this type of critical, engaged, and interdependent learning is quite different from teaching students to perform on a state test. In deliberation, there is rarely a single "correct" outcome, as there may be on a test of knowledge. Similarly, individual students may demonstrate different deliberative skills in different situations, influenced by their own development and the contributions of classmates. Thus, teaching with deliberation requires that educators both understand how public issues can be related to established standards of learning and have the ability to design and facilitate classroom activities that support the enactment and evaluation of deliberative skills over time.

Teaching with deliberation is not a natural process for all teachers. Most teachers are trained in preparation programs that do not explicitly emphasize or use the process of deliberation. In addition, Americans are steeped in a social and political culture that emphasizes a binary approach to thinking about public problems. Policies are framed as either/or: either Democrat or Republican, either liberal or conservative, either right or wrong. Citizens are defined as being either for or against certain policy strategies. In the classroom, this type of thinking is supported by debate-oriented discourse and learning activities that position the teacher as the authority on the curricular topic and on political or social issues.

For teachers, learning to use public deliberation in the classroom is a process of learning to think differently about how to approach course content, how to frame topics and questions in ways that prompt reflection and group analysis, and how to share authority over learning with students. This learning process is supported by ongoing experimentation, reflection, and collaboration with other educators and deliberation practitioners.

Teachers Institutes

In 2008, representatives from NIF-affiliated organizations in Alabama, New York, Pennsylvania, and Wisconsin (a program in Iowa was added in 2011) began to come together in research exchanges convened by the Kettering Foundation to discuss what they were learning in their work with teachers. While the organizations approached their work in different ways, the group concluded that teachers institutes served four common functions for educators:

- introducing teachers to public deliberation and deliberative pedagogy;

- addressing the practical concerns of educators and schools;

- creating a community of educators focused on learning, deliberative practices, and sharing resources;

- building support for their work by linking classroom deliberation to school or community problem solving.

Each center had experience supporting public deliberation in their community, and each center had staff or volunteers with experience working in schools. All of the centers wanted to strengthen their outreach to teachers.

Rather than develop a common training experience for teachers across sites, each center developed its own program for introducing public deliberation to K-12 educators and supporting teachers. Beginning in 2010, the centers wrote and shared reports with one another, and met together each year to reflect on their learning. The fifteen reports they submitted included summaries of what each had done, what they had learned, and what their plans were for maintaining and extending contact with the teachers. Over time, some teachers who were involved in the teachers institutes joined the meetings, sharing their open-ended reports and experiences.

Institutes in Alabama and Pennsylvania focused their work on one or two public school districts and engaged district staff as coleaders of professional development efforts. Institutes on Long Island and in Iowa, both affiliated with university academic departments, connected their efforts to larger initiatives of the university to promote civic learning and advance teacher practice. The Wisconsin Teachers Institute, a project of the Wisconsin Institute for Public Policy and Service (WIPPS) at the University of Wisconsin Marathon County, focused its work on two charter schools and one school district. Nearly all institutes provided some form of follow-up support to teachers after an initial one- or two-day workshop.

This included such things as classroom visits by center staff and opportunities for teachers to participate in learning networks with other teachers. The teachers institutes also connected their work with broader civic-engagement efforts in the community.

Public Deliberation and Deliberative Pedagogy

Learning to use deliberation in the classroom in a sustained way is not something teachers learn from reading an issue guide or attending a single workshop.[68] Learning to teach with deliberation involves developing an understanding of the practice and applying it with students in ways that enhance their ability to work with other citizens to solve problems.

Public deliberation "puts young people into the position of being citizens" by asking them to consider public-policy options and make choices, according to Philip Kane, a teacher at West Islip (New York) High School. Teachers who use the practice need to understand how to engage students as citizens, rather than just students of subject matter.

On Long Island, Michael D'Innocenzo has been working to promote the use of deliberation in the classroom for over 20 years. D'Innocenzo is a retired professor of history at Hofstra University. He is also a founder of the Hofstra Center for Civic Engagement, which hosts the university's teachers institute and many community forums each year. In his 50-plus-year career, D'Innocenzo has played a role in introducing deliberation to countless teachers and citizens through workshops, events, and advocacy. In the 1990s, D'Innocenzo and other educators lobbied the New York legislature to support the establishment of a state-mandated course for teaching the skills of active citizenship in public high schools. A half-credit Participation in Government course is now required in all New York State high schools and provides a space in the formal curricula for institutionalizing public deliberation. In addition, the Hofstra Center for Civic Engagement regularly coordinates projects that link K-12 deliberation to community issues and local and national elections.

D'Innocenzo and his colleague Bernie Stein can provide many examples of how teachers on Long Island have engaged students as citizens by using public deliberation in the Participation in Government courses. Before the teachers introduce deliberation to students, D'Innocenzo and Stein often spend time working with the teachers to introduce them to deliberative citizenship. Stein says one of the most powerful ways of learning about it is by experiencing deliberation as a forum participant. Through this experience, people are able to see and feel how deliberation compares to other forms of dialogue and group learning. If teachers deliberate about a timely public issue as part of their own learning experience, they engage as citizens and begin to recognize the benefits of teaching a form of citizenship that involves making choices.

In addition to experiencing a deliberative forum, it is helpful for teachers to spend time reflecting on the questions, "What is public deliberation?" and "Why should I teach with deliberation?" The first question can be addressed by having educators brainstorm about how deliberation compares to other forms of discourse, such as discussion and debate (see Table 6a). The second question requires more elaboration to lead them to a consideration of both the educational value and the public value of the practice.

"It is important for teachers to understand they are doing something counter-cultural when they teach deliberation. The skills they are teaching are very different from what is modeled on Fox News or MSNBC."

- Bernie Stein

"It is important for teachers to understand that they are doing something counter-cultural when they teach with deliberation," says Stein. "The skills they are teaching are very different from what is modeled on Fox News or MSNBC." When teachers use public deliberation in the classroom, they are teaching a way of talking about public issues that can be a productive alternative to debate.

Table 6a: The Three D's: Discussion, Debate, and Deliberation
(defined by Wisconsin Institute for Public Policy and Service)

Discussion is a relaxed exchange of opinions, characterized by listening to others in order to deepen understanding, maintaining an open-minded attitude, being willing to admit error, searching for basic agreements, maintaining a cordial exchange of ideas, not alienating or offending other participants, and accepting the views of others without questioning or confrontation. The general goals of discussion are to learn more about a particular topic and strengthen interpersonal relationships.

Debate is a focused exploration of two different positions, characterized by searching for weaknesses in the other's position, defending your position, valuing the solution to the problem as more important than the relationship between the debaters, listening closely to find flaws and counter arguments, and seeking to persuade others to accept your viewpoint. The goal of debate is to have a clear winner and loser.

Deliberation is working together to make a decision, characterized by searching for the value in alternate views of the issue, enlarging—and possibly changing—your understanding of the issue, acknowledging that many people have pieces of the answer and that together participants can develop a workable solution, listening to understand the priorities and values of others, and focusing on weighing the benefits and drawbacks of different approaches. The goal of deliberation is to find common ground for action.

Addressing the Practical Concerns of Teachers

Once teachers have experienced deliberation, they can begin to think of ways it can be used in schools to benefit students. At this phase, one important question teachers may ask is, "How can I use public deliberation in the classroom when so much else is expected of me?" As a coleader of the Birmingham Teachers Institute[69] put it, "Teachers have very little time to address the standards outlined by the state department of education. As a result, it proves to be quite difficult for any teacher to implement a new process unless it can be plugged into the [course of study] curriculum." This was a common observation made across teachers institutes, leading convenors to conclude that it was important for them to demonstrate how deliberation can be used to meet Common Core State Standards (CCSS) or other standards adopted by states, such as the College, Career, and Citizenship (C3) Standards of the National Council for Social Studies. Deb Poveromo, social studies department coordinator at State College Area High School, shares a list of CCSS and C3 skills addressed by deliberation in the classroom with teachers. It includes the skills of:

- discussing and evaluating facts linked to controversy;

- determining point of view;

- supporting a point of view with evidence gathered from research;

- listening to opposing points of view and engaging in deliberation;

- proposing solutions to controversial issues;

- collaborating to reach consensus;

- synthesizing information;

- conducting research using several sources.

Reports from teachers suggest that educators appreciated having access to documents that legitimized deliberation's relevance to academic standards. Yet many involved in the teachers institutes raised other practical concerns. They were concerned about issues of classroom management, differentiated instruction, and assessment. They wanted to know how to use deliberation in a "real" classroom. They asked questions like:

- What should I do if a student chooses not to participate or if a student is disruptive?

- How can issue guides be used with students who are reading below grade level?

- What is the best way to evaluate student learning associated with deliberative forums or units?

These issues of classroom practice can contribute to inequalities in learning or cause other problems if not properly addressed. If a few students dominate group activities, or some students are perceived as having a lower status than others, classroom interactions can reinforce prejudices or exacerbate inequalities among students. Ongoing evaluation of the deliberative process and student learning is necessary for teachers to determine if they are meeting the needs of all students. In addition, teachers need to adopt strategies to evaluate the classroom climate and support reflection to limit their own biases in presenting issues.

To address teachers' practice-based concerns, each institute focuses portions of its agenda on addressing common challenges to deliberation in classrooms. One institute, for example, engages teachers in discussions about classroom applications of deliberation and provides specific tips to help teachers anticipate and plan for disruptive students or students who are reluctant to participate. Another emphasizes how carefully worded questions can move a classroom toward more deliberative behaviors. The Iowa Teachers Institute focuses specifically on deliberation as a form of literacy, engaging teachers in consideration of how to use deliberation as a component of effective literacy learning. All of the teachers institutes engage participants in practicing and reflecting on how to moderate a classroom forum.

While a great deal can be learned from quality professional-development workshops, some of the most profound lessons are those that arise when teachers are teaching. Susan Miller's journey with deliberation is a good example of this. Miller is one of a few teachers who participated in the NIF Teachers Network who does not have a background in teaching social studies. A communication arts teacher in an urban district, Miller wanted to use deliberation to teach literacy skills and reinforce the thematic focus of the small learning community in which she taught: public leadership and service.

Miller approached her work with great optimism and enthusiasm. Yet after her first experience with deliberation in the classroom, Miller was disappointed. Although she had a sense that her students had learned something from their experience with deliberation, they struggled to enact a deliberative process. In describing this experience, Miller wrote:

> I think they learned to think for themselves and become better leaders. I think they learned to voice their own opinions and values. I do not think they learned to listen to each other enough or to deliberate effectively. Their deliberations tended to dissolve into debates and had to be stopped at times and restarted.

Rather than engaging the voices of all students and interrogating new perspectives, Miller observed certain students dominating the conversation. Few students referenced others' comments or the NIF issue guide. She realized the skills of conversation and informed reasoning that are important for deliberation are also skills she needed to foster to ensure her students met grade-level standards.

From this experience, Miller concluded that deliberation held promise as a strategy for teaching reading, speaking, and listening skills. But she needed to do more to explicitly teach the basic communication skills required for deliberation if she wanted her students to master them. Her students needed access to the background information to support their critical thinking and speaking, and they needed to learn how to justify their statements using sources. In addition, Miller concluded that she needed to do more to focus her students' attention on the aims of the deliberative process. This would help her reinforce the connection between deliberation and public leadership.

Armed with learning from her first year of experience, Miller dedicated significantly more time to preparing her students for the deliberative process in the second year. She developed her own materials for teaching deliberative skills and she adapted others. She used popular film clips to introduce each issue and integrated research activities into her preforum lessons. She created activities and rubrics to help students focus on the skills of analysis and argumentation.

The result was a deliberative experience that looked more like the forum she had experienced when she deliberated with other teachers. But she still felt she had a lot to learn if she was to become proficient at teaching literacy through deliberation. Such proficiency was essential if she was to receive continued support from her school administrators.

In classrooms, civic-learning goals must coexist alongside the schools' instrumental goals of promoting academic achievement.

Creating a Community of Learners

Susan Miller's experience is quite typical among educators in the NIF network, and suggests, like other classroom practices, that teaching with deliberation involves planning and adaptation by teachers to ensure that all students are learning the intended lessons. This is different from what is expected of deliberation in democracy. Deliberation in democracy aims to promote democratic decision making and advance the public good; it presumes that any group can come together with little preparation to deliberate.

In classrooms, civic-learning goals must coexist alongside the schools' instrumental goals of promoting academic achievement. As a teacher, learning to use deliberation in the classroom involves:

1. committing to learning about and applying deliberative democracy concepts in the classroom;

2. taking steps to create an open class climate where students feel safe to share ideas, even unpopular viewpoints;

3. refining and integrating the practice with other valued teaching practices;

4. empowering students to use the practice, as citizens and learners.

The process of moving from experimentation with deliberation to integrating and cocreating with deliberation is different for every teacher. Some teachers go through common phases of implementation; others do not (see Appendix F). Many teachers report that they benefited from time to reflect and problem solve with other educators. This may be one of the reasons why teachers who worked alone on deliberative experiments were less likely to sustain the practice than teachers who had a partner, or who were active participants in a teachers institute. When teachers worked with another teacher in their school or attended networking sessions, they had opportunities to plan lessons, share ideas, discuss challenges, and be affirmed for the successes that were occurring in their classes, even as they recognized the potential for improvement.

Thus, a core function of the teachers institute is to facilitate connections between teachers to address practice-based concerns and build relationships among teachers to support continued experimentation with deliberation. Networking can occur in different places: at annual summer institutes, day-long learning sessions, classroom-based coaching and coteaching sessions, and after-school meetings. The focus of networking sessions varies according to the needs of the teachers, and includes different configurations, depending on the work to be done. For example, some meetings involve:

- multiple teachers from one school;

- curriculum-based teams across grade levels in a single district;

- teachers who taught similar subjects in different school districts.

In contrast to professional-development models that emphasize the role of expert educators in supporting teacher professional development, teachers institute learning sessions typically involve teachers, teacher educators, community partners, or a community institution (other than the school). Community partners like Peggy Sparks, Michael D'Innocenzo, and Bernie Stein provide concrete examples of how deliberation has been used by citizens. They also mentor teachers who are using deliberation in the classroom and extend opportunities for teachers to connect classroom-based deliberation to similar work within the community. Institutions like universities, museums, and libraries provide community spaces for deliberative experiences, and may partner with teachers on more substantive civic-learning projects.

The David Mathews Center for Civic Life is an example of an institution that has contributed to teacher learning through its involvement in the Birmingham Teachers Institute. The center provides meeting space for teacher workshops, and regularly brings together teachers to frame issues of relevance to the community. For example, in 2010, teachers from Birmingham and other school districts met at the Mathews Center and helped to develop an issue framework on "bullying."[70] Staff at the Mathews Center coordinated the writing, revision, and publication of the issue guide, and hosted test forums at the center. Issue guides were then distributed to teachers for use in schools and communities. Through this experience, teacher-participants learned one approach to framing an issue, and received a valuable resource to support deliberation in their schools. The outcome of this effort was a region-wide discussion in communities and schools about how to deal with the problem of peer abuse. A few years later, the Mathews Center partnered with Alabama Public Television and other sponsors to frame a historical issue guide on civil-rights issues of 1963. Teachers had the opportunity to participate in the framing exercise, and later used the guide and related curriculum resources to commemorate and teach about the issue at the 50-year anniversary of the Selma-to-Montgomery march.[71]

Teachers Institutes: What It Takes

Not all teachers who try to incorporate deliberation in the classroom will continue with the practice. Barriers to continued practice that emerged during this research were related to teachers' classroom management practices and teaching style, school organization, and leadership. Some teachers had difficulty making the shift to a more democratic teaching methodology, finding deliberation incompatible with their approaches to classroom management or subject matter. This may suggest something about the intensity of the professional development offered by the teachers institutes, or it may speak to some educators' resistance to new practices. In other schools, changes in school configuration disrupted teachers' efforts to collaborate in planning deliberative units and network with other teachers. Finally, there were examples of deliberative experiments that ended after changes in school leadership, or when new initiatives were introduced that constrained teachers' autonomy.

Both Kealakehe High School in Kailua CDP, Hawaii, and the School District of Lancaster, in Lancaster, Pennsylvania, received professional development in deliberation from an expert trainer who visited the schools, but was not affiliated with a community institution convening a teachers institute. In each case, teacher training produced deliberative projects; however, the efforts were not sustained in the face of competing priorities, staff turnover, or changes in school leadership.

In the schools that have managed to sustain and deepen their work with deliberation over many years, despite institutional changes, some common elements include:

- an ongoing partnership with an organization that convenes deliberative forums in the community;

- sustained learning opportunities for teachers;

- on-site coaching and support by a skilled facilitator;

- validation/recognition of teachers and schools.

In Wisconsin, John Greenwood has played an important role in supporting teacher success with deliberation through his role as outreach coordinator at the Wisconsin Institute for Public Policy and Service. His work with teachers includes most of the elements listed above. Yet unlike leaders from other teachers institutes, Greenwood did not have a clear idea of where deliberation would fit or how it would be used when he began working with schools. This openness allowed him to listen to educators' goals and consider ways that deliberation, as a democratic practice, could contribute to the educational agenda that already existed. From this approach, three different deliberative projects emerged. One focused on the use of deliberative decision making to improve school climate and governance of the school; another focused on using deliberation to teach global issues and perspective-taking; and a third focused on supporting the social and civic development of children at risk of school failure.

During a visit to Wausau, Wisconsin, I was surprised to see the diverse ways in which the schools had embraced deliberative teaching practices and had begun to fold them into their own structures and routines. Deliberation had become more than a teaching strategy; it had become a way of organizing the work of the schools and fostering relationships among staff and students.

Sarah Schneck, one of the first teachers you met in this book, helped develop the deliberative project at Enrich, Excel, Achieve Learning Academy. Her principal spoke of her school's commitment to deliberation in this way: "Changes in education are almost guaranteed . . . but we are not turning back from deliberation." Deliberation had become too important for her students. To illustrate this point, she shared a story of how students had used deliberation to face a tragic and potentially divisive issue in the community.

Two weeks before I visited EEA, there had been a student death in the community. A disagreement had broken out after school among rival groups of students. One group of students travelled to another student's home, where a fight ensued. Weapons were drawn; a student was stabbed and later died. Because some of the involved students were lifelong residents of Wausau, nearly every high school student in the community had some connection to the tragedy. The principal described how disruptive the event had been at her daughter's traditional high school. In the days following the fight, rumors circulated, and students were emotional and distracted from their schoolwork.

The reaction at EEA was markedly different, according to Schneck. "Our kids were upset, but they didn't show it. They went through their day, did their work, and stayed on task. There was no drama. . . . They waited until they got to deliberation class and that is where they dealt with it."

Both Schneck and the principal described how the students, visibly upset, processed the tragedy with peers who had been their partners in deliberation for more than a year. They talked about what they had read and heard about the event, listened to each other, carefully stated their concerns, and linked the conversation to the choices that had been studied when the class deliberated about youth violence a month earlier.

I was so impressed by how sensitive they were to each other," Schneck noted. "They chose their words carefully. . . . They were just so respectful and everyone supported each other."

The students at EEA had developed the capacity, as a community, to face an unspeakable tragedy together. They were not concerned with laying blame or distracted by the media hype. They wanted to support each other and they wanted to talk about what they and their community could do to address a public problem. They had a vocabulary for talking about the issue, and they had the ability to work together in the face of uncertainty because they were in the habit of deliberating. Mostly, though, they were acting as citizens—citizens who have a stake in their community, and who are committed to working together to claim a better future.

Isn't that what democracy and public education are all about?

AFTERWORD

....

I especially enjoyed writing this piece for Stacie's book because I have a personal connection to the subject. I come from a family of teachers: my grandfather, both of my parents, an aunt and an uncle, my cousins, and on to the next generation. When I was a college student, my goal was to be a history teacher. I earned a PhD from Columbia University with that in mind. And when I took my first job after graduation, even though it was in university administration, I insisted on teaching at least one history class. I continued to teach every year until I left academe for the job I have now at a research foundation, Kettering. My colleagues there say that I still try to find a way to teach. I am not sure whether that is a compliment or a complaint, but I take it as a compliment.

Teaching is the most rewarding and the most challenging thing I've ever done — with the exception of having to grade papers, which I haven't found so rewarding. Teaching demands every bit of imagination and creativity that I can muster in trying to engage students and young research assistants, who are not always as interested in history as I am.

Teachers have to keep searching for better ways to teach. *Deliberation in the Classroom* is about a group of teachers and what they have found so far in their search, which has revolutionized their classes. They want to share what they are doing and, if you are interested, they want you to join them in an experimental approach to teaching that could help revitalize the classroom. The classroom has become burdened by too much emphasis on testing, by well-intentioned but misguided attempts to use quantitative measures for things that are quintessentially qualitative, and by an overabundance of bureaucratic rigidity, standardization, and lack of autonomy. Worst of all, many teachers say they are afraid to experiment because they will be penalized for failing. That's tragic because innovation requires learning from failures — learning to "fail intelligently," which was one of the mantras of the inventor Charles Kettering.

This book tells the stories of teachers who are helping young people learn how to live among, and work with, others who aren't like them, and who may not particularly care for them. Their students learn how to deal with conflicting points of view, and how to make good choices together that will shape their future and the future of the places where they will live and pursue their careers. Although in different fields, all of these teachers have been engaging their students in making collective decisions to combat problems they face now and will face when they graduate. They are teaching Living 101. The issues students grapple with in their classes are about what they should or shouldn't do as a student body, as members of a community, as citizens. These "should" questions are normative; there is not one certain, objective answer that will suit everyone. Facts are important, yet there are no experts on normative questions. Dealing constructively with them requires dealing with differences of opinions, which are inescapable. And this requires that students exercise their faculty for judgment. Judgment arises from the deliberative thinking that is used in making sound decisions on normative issues.

In the classes described in these pages, students have serious work to do. They aren't on the sidelines watching; they are leading the deliberative decision making in their classes. They have to work their way through tough-to-make choices, not to the point where everyone agrees, but to the point where the class has identified ways of moving forward on a problem, ways that most everyone can live with even if they aren't fully satisfied. That's a key to democratic problem solving in a diverse society.

The teachers described here teach what has been called "choice work" by some, and deliberative decision making by others. Whatever the term, the goal is to get young people to use the part of their brains that helps them make the best possible decisions when faced with the uncertainty that is part of life at any age. In some classes, teachers use contemporary issues like dealing with violence in the school and community. In other classes, the deliberations are on historical decisions, perhaps going as far back as the question of whether to become an independent country. Teachers are introducing history, not as inevitability, but rather as a matter of choices. Even though the issue may be historical, the students have little difficulty in recognizing the implications of what they are studying for their lives today. That's a big plus in teaching. Students are learning how to think—and how to think with other people. I was particularly impressed to find that students who have difficulty relating to conventional classroom instruction often respond well in classes where they are involved in choice work.

Using choice work to teach is not a methodology or formula. Life is a series of choices—individual, professional, and collective—and in all cases, deeply personal. Having students wrestle with making difficult decisions requires teachers to step back enough for students to engage one another so that deliberation occurs. However, as the deliberations end, teachers reenter the class to guide students' reflections on what they learned from the experience and on the implications for the subject they are studying. Some call this teaching through deliberation "deliberative pedagogy," a term coined by university faculty members who also use choice work in their classes. There are as many types of deliberative pedagogy as there are classes because it is an experimental approach to teaching. Different issues produce different classroom deliberations and no two classrooms are the same because students differ.

Although the book only covers secondary school and one fifth-grade class, other studies show that even younger children have an aptitude for deliberating. In an experiment with students in kindergarten through second grade, a researcher, Dr. Kim Pearce, has reported that children developed "the ability to see and describe pros and cons of each choice, to think about trade-offs, and possibly even change their mind(s)."[72]

What students learn from choice work is subject matter, but much more. They discover their own inherent powers of agency. They learn how to make a difference in their world. They know how to be citizens, not just on Election Day, but every day and everywhere collective decisions have to be made—in their organizations, on their sports teams, even in their homes with siblings. Furthermore, at a time when many Americans doubt that they can make a difference in our political system, a civics course that teaches agency, and not just how a bill is passed, is invaluable.

I hope this book will contribute to what is already happening without any central direction or external support. Teachers from different parts of the country have created networks (loose associations) of the kind characteristic of inventors. That is, they are talking to one another and comparing experiences. As I said initially, these teachers welcome anyone who wants to join in these exchanges, which already extend beyond the United States. The National Issues Forums Institute, www.nifi.org, will be happy to direct you to these teachers.

David Mathews
President
Kettering Foundation

APPENDICES

APPENDIX A
NIF Issue Framework *1776: What Should We Do?*

Three Options for the Second Continental Congress

Option 1 of 3	What We Should Do	Drawbacks
REMAIN LOYAL TO BRITAIN'S KING The colonists should be true to their heritage and remember that people in the 13 colonies are subjects of The Crown.	Break up the Continental Army, denounce the actions of the militias, and call for the Sons of Liberty and other protest groups to disband.	Even if we do this, the feelings that led to the formation of the Sons of Liberty and the colonial militias will not simply disappear. Violence may well break out again.
The colonies are a proud part of the powerful British Empire. They share a common language and traditions. Their laws and rights come from the mother country. The religious faith of most people in the colonies and in Britain is similar.	Call for an end to all boycotts, and urge merchants to continue (or resume) trading with Britain.	Commerce in the colonies is one of the chief ways for Britain to pay for the expenses of running its empire. So colonial businesses will continue to be highly taxed.
The people in the colonies have prospered economically and enjoy the protection of the British army. It would be both wrong and foolish for the colonies to rebel and break away from the mother country.	Urge people to identify and turn in those who have led and supported the rebels.	The rebellion has widespread support. This course of action will pit colony against colony, colonist against colonist. It may split families and cause friends and neighbors to take up arms against one another.

Voices from History

Obedience to government is every man's duty, because it is every man's interest; but it is particularly incumbent on Christians, because (in addition to its moral fitness) it is enjoined by the positive commands of God; and, therefore, when Christians are disobedient to human ordinances, they are also disobedient to God.

—Jonathan Boucher, final American sermon in 1775

Three Options for the Second Continental Congress

Option 2 of 3

DECLARE INDEPENDENCE IN CLEAR TERMS

The colonists can be bold and declare that the 13 colonies are independent states.

Britain's government has steadily stripped colonists of their traditional liberties and inherent rights, acting against their British heritage and the natural law. There can be no lasting peace nor economic prosperity without guarantees for the colonists' rights to liberty.

The 13 colonies should declare their independence and establish a confederacy, the United States of America. The people of these united states should pledge to cooperate for their common defense and accept whatever consequences this may bring.

Voices from History

We have done everything that could be done to avert the storm which is now coming on. We have petitioned; we have remonstrated; we have supplicated; we have prostrated ourselves before the throne. … There is no longer any room for hope.… Give me liberty or give me death.

—Patrick Henry, to the Second Virginia Convention, March 23, 1775

What We Should Do	Drawbacks
Declare that the colonies in America are independent, and draft Articles of Confederation to preserve the sovereign rights and independence of each state in these United States of America.	Such a move will permanently separate the colonies from the United Kingdom of Great Britain and lead to a war with an outcome that is uncertain. The colonies will almost certainly require support from the French or other British enemies, which they are unlikely to get. The new, loosely joined confederacy may have trouble agreeing on important decisions.
Ask the colonies to continue to provide soldiers for the Continental Army.	The army will necessarily be weak, as it will depend on volunteers, on funding from General Washington and other wealthy patriots, and on taxes beyond what most people can manage. If this effort fails, leaders and soldiers will be hanged as traitors.
Require that businesses cut off all trade with Britain.	This loss will surely drive many colonial businesses into ruin.

Three Options for the Second Continental Congress

Option 3 of 3

USE DIPLOMACY TO ADVANCE COLONISTS' AIMS WITHIN THE BRITISH EMPIRE

The colonists can negotiate a peaceful solution.

The colonies have valid grievances that can be solved without military conflict. The colonies are not ready for complete independence. They might fail if they tried independence.

The main grievance is the lack of representation in Parliament. The colonies should form an American Parliament, made up of representatives from the various colonies, to work in partnership with the British Parliament. New laws and policies for America would require the agreement of both American and British Parliaments.

Meanwhile, the colonies should build up their military and economic strength and seek friendlier relations with traditional British foes, such as France and Spain, in case diplomacy fails.

Voices from History

Let us ask for a participation in the freedom and power of the English constitution in some other mode of incorporation ... and as you wish to avoid a war with Great Britain, which must terminate, at all events in the ruin of America, not to rely on a denial of the authority of Parliament.

—Joseph Galloway to the First Continental Congress, September 28, 1774

What We Should Do	Drawbacks
Establish an American legislature that would work with the British Parliament to make the colonies a confederation of locally self-governing states within the authority of the United Kingdom of Great Britain.	People in the colonies will continue to be subject to the decisions of the British Parliament and king, far away across the Atlantic Ocean.
Work toward changing the views of the British Parliament, relying on the advice of prominent British political leaders who are open to a fairer relationship between the Crown and its colonies.	Supporters in Parliament won't guarantee that the colonies will be treated fairly. Britons sympathetic to the colonies may remain a minority, and the majority may still force their will on the colonies.
Seek to improve relations with France, Spain, and other long-standing British enemies, so that if war does come, the colonies will not have to face Great Britain alone.	Word of these moves may get out, causing Britain to punish the colonies even more. In addition, the four colonies of New England, which feel grievances more strongly than the other nine colonies, could declare independence apart from the others and weaken the position of the remaining nine.

APPENDIX B		
Educator-Developed Issue Framework *Bullying: How Do We Prevent It?*		
Three Options for Preventing Bullying		
Option 1 of 3	**What We Should Do**	**Drawbacks**
GET TOUGH ON BULLIES Bullying is unacceptable. It must be treated with zero tolerance. Increased reports of bullying in our schools demand that teachers, principals, and school districts do more to help prevent bullying and provide tougher consequences for those who engage in it. We must ensure that school districts' anti-harassment policies and student codes of conduct are in place and strictly enforced.	Implement zero-tolerance policies and procedures.	Zero-tolerance policies may push some students out of school prematurely.
	Establish tougher consequences for bullying in student codes of conduct, to communicate clearly that bullying is unacceptable.	Imposing tougher consequences ignores the underlying issues that cause young people to bully.
	Station police officers in schools to reinforce that bullying and violence have severe consequences.	Police efforts should focus on criminal behavior outside of the schools. Stationing police officers in every school would be costly.
	Require teachers and staff members to report bullying within 24 hours of an incident.	Teachers may feel compelled to submit formal bullying reports even for minor playground spats; overreacting may create more problems.
	Emphasize the need for bystanders to communicate that bullying is unacceptable. Teach young people what to do when they witness bullying.	Those who intervene may become victims of cyberbullying or other forms of revenge and harassment.

Three Options for Preventing Bullying

Option 2 of 3	What We Should Do	Drawbacks
EQUIP SCHOOLS TO ADDRESS BULLYING Not every young person understands what constitutes bullying or how to respond to it. We need to educate children about bullying and effective ways to deal with it. Many feel powerless as victims or as bystanders. At the same time, many bullies do not understand the effects of their actions. The lines between victims and bullies often become blurred when circumstances change or victims retaliate. We should create supportive, enriching school cultures that equip teachers, staff, and students to address the root causes of bullying.	Establish a school-wide information program about bullying that includes self-confidence training, to teach young people how to respond to bullies.	Forceful actions by victims could bring them greater torment from bullies.
	Make sure that young people know whom they should contact if bullying occurs.	Teachers and other school personnel do not have the time and resources to adequately address every instance of bullying.
	Encourage peaceful solutions and peer mediation programs to help bullies build social skills.	Without tough consequences for bullies, young people may not take the problem seriously.*
	Educate school counselors, teachers, staff, coaches, and administrators to address the root causes of bullying and to serve as role models for positive interactions.	Addressing the complex root causes of bullying is best left to the expertise of mental health and behavioral professionals.
	Create a culture of respect in our schools.	It is the responsibility of parents and community members to determine moral standards and encourage strong character in young people.

Author's note: Also, students who are bullied may continue to be harmed if peer mediation, rather than adult intervention, is used to address bullying problems.

Three Options for Preventing Bullying

Option 3 of 3	What We Should Do	Drawbacks
ENGAGE THE COMMUNITY AND PARENTS IN PREVENTING BULLYING Bullying is a widespread behavior that is not limited to educational settings, so schools should not bear the entire responsibility for addressing this public health issue. Parents and community members should discuss bullying and think of ways to prevent it. A lot of bullying and violent behavior begins at home. We must reach out to parents and to young people, some of whom need community help because they do not have a supportive home environment.	Encourage greater parental monitoring of children's cell phones and Internet use, and promote policies for acceptable use of social media and the Internet.	This requires parents to spend much more time and energy monitoring their children, time that some parents do not have. Such monitoring is also an invasion of children's privacy.
	Conduct presentations at PTA and community meetings about the nature, impact, and warning signs of bullying.	These meetings may not reach people in troubled homes or those who are too busy to attend.
	Address bullying prevention through service projects and meetings coordinated by civic groups and businesses.	These meetings and projects may not reach many of the people who need them.
	Train community members and parents to identify the signs that a child is bullying or being bullied.	Schools, not the community, should be responsible for addressing the problem, as most childhood bullying occurs in the school environment.
	Encourage community mentoring and character education programs to reinforce positive behavior and prevent bullying.	Focusing on mentoring and character education may result in neglecting other important community problems.

APPENDIX C
Teaching Tools and Strategies

Starter Videos

Many NIF issue guides have accompanying starter videos. These videos, which are 7-12 minutes in length, introduce the issue and the three options described in the issue guide. Teachers use the videos early in a class unit to introduce the issue guide, or use segments of the videos to introduce individual options as part of classroom forums. The video gives students a summary of key facts and vocabulary. (For more information, go to www.nifi.org.)

Issue "Deconstruction" Worksheets

Issue deconstruction refers to the process of breaking down issue guides into common components as a way of focusing students' attention on key ideas. Consistent with the practice of providing a "reading guide"* to support a student's comprehension of text, an issue deconstruction worksheet focuses students' attention on key information within the issue guide and within each option, including evidence that the issue is a problem, action proposed, and trade-offs. (See Appendix D: Issue Deconstruction Worksheet). Some teachers may assign the guides as homework, while others will have students complete the guides in class, independently or in groups.

Jigsaw Assignments

The jigsaw technique is a way of teaching that improves cooperation and learning in diverse classrooms. In essence, the strategy involves breaking assignments into chunks and asking students to master portions of the material and teach it to others. In classes that use deliberation, teachers will often assign students one option to learn and master from an issue guide. Students may complete part of an issue deconstruction guide, conduct additional online research that supports their assigned option, or conduct interviews with parents and neighbors to gain their perspective on that option. Then, individuals or groups of students present the option to the class, focusing on key ideas and facts, proposed actions, benefits, and trade-offs. (For more information on the jigsaw technique, go to www.jigsaw.org.)

Partner Reading

Partner reading involves placing students in pairs and assigning oral reading to the small groups. As a student reads aloud, his or her partner is available to "listen, follow along, or provide needed words or assistance."** Students switch roles periodically, allowing the reader to become the listener and support, as needed.

Annotation

Annotation is way to promote active reading and comprehension of text. Students are encouraged to write thoughts and questions—often on the margins of the page or in a notebook—as they read or reread text.*** Before they begin reading, students may leaf through the book or article and write questions they have about the topic or predictions about the text. While reading the text, students are encouraged to underline, highlight, and use specific symbols to indicate main idea, characters, vocabulary, etc. They are also encouraged to summarize what they have read and document any connections that they might have to the text (such as personal experience, current events, or other texts). When they finish reading, the annotations they have recorded may be useful in helping them draw conclusions or recall key facts about what they have read.

*Reading guides often mirror specific comprehension strategies teachers are reinforcing with students. They may focus on content, interpretation, application, or other aspects of comprehension. For examples, see http://www.readingeducator.com/strategies/three.htm.

** Elizabeth Meisinger, et al., "Interaction Quality During Partner Reading," *Journal of Literacy Research* 36, no.2 (2004), 111-140.

***For more information, see Carol Porter-O'Donnell, "Beyond the Yellow Highlighter: Teaching Annotation Skills to Improve Reading Comprehension," *English Journal* 93, no. 5 (May 2004), 82-89.

APPENDIX D				
Issue Deconstruction Worksheet				
Issue/Title:				
Approach/Option Name	According to this approach, the real problem is:	To address the issue/problem, we should:	Possible positive consequences of these actions	Possible drawbacks and trade-offs
1.				
2.				
3.				

APPENDIX E
Historic Decisions and Related Resources

1776: What Should We Do?
Before the Declaration of Independence
NIF Historic Decisions
www.nifi.org

A New Land: What Kind of Government Should We Have?
Before the Constitutional Congress, 1787
NIF Historic Decisions
www.nifi.org

Slavery or Freedom Forever: What's at Stake in the Kansas-Nebraska Act?
Before passage of the Kansas-Nebraska Act, 1854
New England Center for Public Life (Douglas A. Ley, author, Joni Doherty, editor)
www.nifi.org

What Should the United States Do About the Emerging Threat Posed by the Soviet Union?
Harry Truman's foreign policy options, 1947
National Archives' Advise the President Series: Harry S. Truman
https://www.advisethepresident.archives.gov/booklets

How Should the United States Confront Soviet Communist Expansionism?
Dwight Eisenhower's foreign policy options, 1953
National Archives' Advise the President Series: Dwight D. Eisenhower
https://www.advisethepresident.archives.gov/booklets

How Should the United States Move Toward Economic Recovery?
Ronald Reagan's economic policy options, 1981
National Archives' Advise the President Series: Ronald Reagan
https://www.advisethepresident.archives.gov/booklets

How Should the Federal Government Respond to New York City's Financial Crisis?
Gerald Ford's options for responding to New York City's economic crisis, 1975
National Archives' Advise the President Series: Gerald R. Ford
https://www.advisethepresident.archives.gov/booklets

What Should the United States Do About the Kosovo Crisis?
Bill Clinton's foreign policy options, 1999
National Archives' Advise the President Series: William J. Clinton
https://www.advisethepresident.archives.gov/booklets

APPENDIX F
Learning to Use Public Deliberation in the Classroom with NIF:
Some Common Phases

Phase 1: Experimentation	Common Activities:	Students' Response:	Teacher Adaptation/ Response:
When teachers first use NIF and deliberation with students, they may feel uncertain about the process and what students are learning.	Teachers frequently use instigating activities to bring students into the issue. This may include videos, editorials, current events articles, cartoons, etc. A whole class deliberation is conducted using a 90-100 minute block of time. Teachers act as moderators, using predetermined questions (such as NIF questions) to promote deliberation. Post-forum reflection is the primary method of evaluation.	Increased student engagement is observed, particularly among students who tend not to participate/lead. There may be a tendency for a few students to dominate the conversation. Students may share personal experiences and opinions, but may not justify claims by referencing specific text. Student reflection focuses on the issue and their connection to it.	After the initial experience with deliberation, teachers may struggle to judge whether the process was a success. In preparing for a second deliberative forum, teachers may decide to focus on teaching deliberative communication skills explicitly. They may also develop formative or summative assessments that focus on issue-specific vocabulary and writing.

APPENDIX F
Learning to Use Public Deliberation in the Classroom with NIF:
Some Common Phases

Phase 2: Refinement	Common Activities:	Students' Response:	Teacher Adaptation/ Response:
Early in teachers' use of deliberation, they begin to make connections between NIF, deliberation, and academic standards. Teachers become more aware of what deliberation looks like and experiment with ways of promoting it.	Teachers may break students into jigsaw groups in preparation for the forum. After initial preparation, the forum may be conducted over 2-3 days (45-minute classes). Teachers become more comfortable with generating their own questions and probing to support deliberation. Teachers provide more explicit activities on what deliberation is, why it is important, and what it looks like. It is common to see the use of discussion rubrics at this phase. Teachers experiment with different reflection activities/ assignments to assess learning.	Teachers may witness more students participating, now that students understand the process and how they will be assessed. Students improve in their ability to communicate, disagree respectfully, and think interdependently. Minority perspectives may be stifled at times. Students are able to focus on the issue and the deliberative process. Common ground for action may be evident.	Teachers begin to become more conscious of the academic and civic learning that deliberation can support. Teachers understand and recognize new ways of using deliberation and deliberative concepts (tension, trade-offs, common ground) in their classrooms. Teachers are cognizant of the need to ensure that the best argument for each choice is put forth. Teachers consciously plan to ensure minority perspectives are protected/heard. The question, "Whose voice is not in the room?" may be introduced.

APPENDIX F
Learning to Use Public Deliberation in the Classroom with NIF:
Some Common Phases

Phase 3: Integration	Common Activities:	Students' Response:	Teacher Adaptation/ Response:
Through experience, teachers have a deeper understanding of what deliberation is and what it aims to accomplish. They are able to re-appropriate the process and concepts in their classrooms and extracurricular work with students.	Teachers plan and use forums, deliberative questioning, and deliberative concepts as an integrated part of their teaching. Teachers name and frame topics in their curriculum to enrich learning and draw connections between curriculum and choice work. Example: An Alabama teacher reframed a civil rights unit by focusing on the very different perspectives of three civil rights leaders. Students studied these perspectives using primary and secondary sources and then deliberated as if they were policy options.	Higher-order communication and thinking skills are evident. Students are able to recognize that how an issue is framed can influence how we talk, think, learn, and act. Students begin seeking additional perspectives on topics they are studying OR recognize when a voice is not represented. Students may want to frame their own issues.	The class and teacher become more concerned with how deliberation connects to democratic social change. Teachers look for ways to link classroom deliberation to civic action. Teachers may plan follow-up activities that involve service, communicating with elected officials, advocacy, etc. Teachers work hard to maintain space for diverse perspectives and actions among students. The concept of "complementary action" may be explored.

APPENDIX F
Learning to Use Public Deliberation in the Classroom with NIF:
Some Common Phases

Phase 4: Co-creation	Common Activities:	Students' Response:	Teacher Adaptation/ Response:
Teachers begin to share ownership of the deliberative process with students.	Students identify issues in the school/ community.	Students can identify the many stakeholders affected by an issue, including those not typically highlighted in mainstream media.	Teachers serve as partners, coaches, and supporters of citizen-students.
	Students are taught methods of framing and moderating.		Adults may work to facilitate opportunities for students to host forums in the school/community.
	Teachers support students in naming and framing their own issues and as they test and revise their issue frameworks.	Students conduct research on the issue with a focus on exploring the many ways it is experienced, understood, written about, and discussed.	Teachers may integrate student-framed issues into the curricula for future classes.
	Students conduct traditional research and interview citizens to learn about the issue and people's concerns.	Students are able to frame their own issues and write issue guides.	
		Students may moderate forums in their schools and/or communities.	

APPENDIX G
Explanation of Terms

Common ground is the mutual understanding among people that can result from participating in a deliberative discussion. Common ground may include areas of agreed understanding and/or a mutual understanding of differences, and can be the basis for public action.

Deliberation is a way people can make decisions, both individually and in groups, that are rooted in the things citizens hold valuable. It is the practice of carefully weighing options for action and considering trade-offs in order to decide what should be done. Sometimes this is called choice work.

A *deliberative forum* is a structured way for groups of citizens to discuss a community issue. It involves a careful consideration of the actions, drawbacks, and trade-offs associated with three or more proposed options for addressing an issue.

A *forum moderator* is an impartial facilitator who works to ensure that deliberation occurs by maintaining a focus on the options, posing questions to prompt deliberation and reflection, and ensuring the group adheres to the chosen rules of behavior, but who does not otherwise participate in the forum discussion.

Framing is the process of collecting and presenting three or more options for acting on a problem or issue. It includes diverse perspectives used to understand the issue or problem, as well as critical information, drawbacks, and trade-offs associated with each option.

An *issue framework* is an abbreviated document that presents an issue for deliberation. It is often designed as a grid that includes the name of the problem and brief information about each option, as well as a few possible actions, drawbacks, and potential trade-offs.

An *issue guide* is an expanded version of the issue framework that includes additional background information, statistics, and key facts on the issue and detailed descriptions of potential actions, drawbacks, and trade-offs.

Naming refers to the way a problem or issue is identified or introduced, and may be posed in the form of a question. The name given to a problem influences how it is discussed, as well as the range of ideas, facts, and options that are considered.

Politics is the way people work together to meet community needs and solve community problems. It includes how members of the community relate to each other and proceed when faced with a problem, as well as what governments and elected officials do.

Prescriptive framings direct students or citizens to a predetermined or preferred outcome, and may limit the range of options or perspectives considered.

Public deliberation is a specific type of group deliberation focused on deciding what should be done to solve public issues.

Public issues are complex, persistent problems that are difficult for communities to solve and that affect groups of people differently. Public issues cannot be solved by individuals or groups alone. Making progress on public issues requires individual, group, and institutional attention and action over time.

Reframing the curriculum is a term used by many educators who teach with deliberation in the classroom. It describes the intentional decision by the teacher to present curricular content in a way that fosters deliberation by increasing students' exposure to diverse perspectives, choices, and trade-offs that are inherent within a topic of study.

Trade-offs are things that citizens must give-up if a particular course of action is pursued. Trade-offs are consequences that affect the things people value if a particular decision is made.

NOTES AND BIBLIOGRAPHY

Notes

Chapter One

[1] For more information about political polarization in America, see Tom David, et al., *The Partisan Divide* (Campbell, CA: FastPencil Premiere, 2014) and Nate Cohn, "Polarization Is Dividing American Society, Not Just Politics" (*New York Times*, June 12, 2014).

[2] In the book *Building America*, Boyte and Kari define public work as "work that makes things of value and importance, in cooperation with others" (Philadelphia: Temple University Press, 1996), 2.

[3] For more information about deliberation in communities, see David Mathews, *For Communities to Work* (Kettering Foundation Press, 2002). For a more theoretical review of the role of deliberation in democracy, see *Why Deliberative Democracy?* by Amy Gutmann and Dennis Thompson (Princeton University Press, 2004).

[4] The phrase "current, relevant, real world" was used by Patricia Avery, et al. to describe topics suited for deliberation; see Patricia G. Avery, et al., *The Expanding Deliberating in a Democracy (Did) Project Evaluation Report: Year 1 Project Narrative*, http://www.did.deliberating.org/about_us/documents/Expanding%20DID%20Year%201%20(07-08)%20Evaluation.pdf (accessed December 6, 2016).

[5] This definition was adapted from a description of classroom deliberation provided by Joni Doherty in *Individual and Community: Deliberative Practices in a First-Year Seminar* (2004), https://www.kettering.org/sites/default/files/product-downloads/JoniDohertyIndividual_0.pdf (accessed October 3, 2016).

[6] Abdelkader Benali, "From Teenage Angst to Jihad" (*New York Times*, January 13, 2015), http://www.nytimes.com/2015/01/14/opinion/the-anger-of-europes-young-marginalized-muslims.html?_r=0 (accessed October 3, 2016).

[7] Some examples of civic education programs that foster engagement with current events include Kids Voting USA, Newscurrents, The Choices Program, and the Classroom Close-up curriculum.

[8] Research suggests that alienation plays a role in student disengagement from school and can make students more vulnerable to bullying and other forms of peer aggression; see Tina Hascher and Gerda Hagenauer, "Alienation from School," *International Journal of Educational Research* 49, no. 6 (2010), 220-232; Lisa Legault, Isabelle Green-Demers, and Luc Pelletier, "Why Do High School Students Lack Motivation in the Classroom?" *Journal of Educational Psychology* 98, no. 3 (2006), 567; Kipling Williams, Joseph Forgas, and William von Hippel, eds., *The Social Outcast: Ostracism, Social Exclusion, Rejection, and Bullying* (New York: Psychology Press, 2005).

[9] The National Issues Forums Institute (NIFI) is a nonprofit, nonpartisan organization that serves to promote public deliberation and coordinate the activities of the National Issues Forums network. Its activities include publishing the issue guides and other materials used by local forum groups, encouraging collaboration among forum sponsors, and sharing information about current activities in the network.

Chapter Two

[10] Amy Gutmann and Dennis Thompson, *Why Deliberative Democracy?* (Princeton, NJ: Princeton University Press, 2004).

[11] Numerous studies document the importance of having a safe or "open" classroom climate for students to learn from deliberation. For more information, see Patricia Avery, "Teaching Tolerance: What Research Tells Us," *Social Education* 66, no. 5 (2002), 270-275; Carole Hahn and Cynthia Tocci, "Classroom Climate and Controversial Issues Discussions: A Five Nation Study," *Theory and Research in Social Education* 18, no. 4 (1990), 344-362; and Deborah Cotton, "Teaching Controversial Environmental Issues: Neutrality and Balance in the Reality of the Classroom," *Educational Research* 48, no. 2 (2006), 223-224.

[12] See Jonathan Gould, ed., *Guardian of Democracy: The Civic Mission of Schools*, The Leonore Annenberg Institute for Civics of the Annenberg Public Policy Center at the University of Pennsylvania and the Campaign for the Civic Mission of Schools, http://civicmission. s3.amazonaws.com/118/f0/5/171/1/Guardian-of-Democracy-report.pdf (accessed October 3, 2016).

[13] "Participation and Deliberation" is defined as a series of outcomes within the C3 Civics domain. See National Council for the Social Studies (NCSS), *The College, Career, and Civic Life (C3) Framework for Social Studies State Standards: Guidance for Enhancing the Rigor of K-12 Civics, Economics, Geography, and History* (Silver Spring, MD: NCSS, 2013), http://www. socialstudies.org/system/files/c3/C3-Framework-for-Social-Studies.pdf (accessed October 3, 2016).

[14] National Council for the Social Studies (NCSS), *The College, Career, and Civic Life (C3) Framework*, 19.

[15] Arthur L. Costa and Bena Kallick, eds., *Learning and Leading with Habits of Mind: 16 Essential Characteristics for Success* (Alexandria, VA: Association for Supervision and Curriculum Development, 2008).

[16] Sarah Michaels, Catherine O'Connor, and Lauren B. Resnick, "Deliberative Discourse Idealized and Realized: Accountable Talk in the Classroom and in Civic Life," *Studies in Philosophy and Education* 27, no. 4 (2008), 283-297.

[17] Sarah Michaels, Richard Sohmer, and Mary C. O'Connor, "Discourse in the Classroom," in Herausgegeben von Ulrich Ammon, et al., eds., *Sociolinguistics: An International Handbook of the Science of Language and Society*, 2nd edition (New York: Walter de Gruyter, 2004), 2351-2366.

[18] Catherine Bitter, et al., "What Works to Improve Student Literacy Achievement? An Examination of Instructional Practices in a Balanced Literacy Approach," *Journal of Education for Students Placed at Risk* 14, no. 1 (2009), 17-44; Penny Howell, Shelley Thomas, and Yuliya Ardasheva, "Talk in the Classroom: Meeting the Developmental, Academic, and Cultural Needs of Middle School Students," *Middle Grades Research Journal* 6, no. 1 (2011), 47-63.

[19] The rationale for teaching noncognitive skills is well articulated by the Collaborative for Social and Emotional Learning (CASEL), www.casel.org. For additional reading, see Daniel Goleman, *Emotional Intelligence* (New York: Bantam, 2006); Mark A. Brackett, Susan E. Rivers, and Peter Salovey, "Emotional Intelligence: Implications for Personal, Social, Academic, and Workplace Success," *Social and Personality Psychology Compass* 5, no. 1 (2011), 88-103.

[20] Noncognitive skills have been defined in different ways in the literature and include such things as social skills, persistence, tenacity, empathy, and problem-solving skills. The construct of "grit" by Angela Duckworth, et al., is another example. ("Grit: Perseverance and Passion for Long-Term Goals," *Journal of Personality and Social Psychology* 92, no. 6 [2007], 1087). The book *How Children Succeed: Grit, Curiosity, and the Hidden Power of Character* by Paul Tough (First Mariner Books, 2013) provides an overview of this research and its relevance to life outcomes.

[21] Paul Tough, *How Children Succeed*; Angela L. Duckworth, et al., "Grit: Perseverance and Passion for Long-Term Goals"; Deborah Cobb-Clark and Michele Tan, "Noncognitive Skills, Occupational Attainment, and Relative Wages," *Labour Economics* 18, no. 1 (2011), 1-13; James Heckman and Yona Rubinstein, "The Importance of Noncognitive Skills: Lessons from the GED Testing Program," *American Economic Review* 19, no. 2 (2001), 145-149.

[22] Dustin Albert and Laurence Steinberg, "Judgment and Decision Making in Adolescence," *Journal of Research on Adolescence* 21, no. 1 (2011), 211-224.

[23] Ibid, 15-16.

[24] John W. Payton, et al., "Social and Emotional Learning: A Framework for Promoting Mental Health and Reducing Risk Behavior in Children and Youth," *Journal of School Health* 70, no. 5 (2000), 179-185.

[25] Joseph Durlak, et al., "The Impact of Enhancing Students' Social and Emotional Learning: A Meta Analysis of School Based Universal Interventions," *Child Development* 82, no. 1 (2011), 405-432. Students who experienced explicit SEL instruction scored 11 percentage points higher on achievement tests.

[26] Student names have been changed to protect their identity.

[27] Horst W. J. Rittel and Melvin M. Webber, "Dilemmas in a General Theory of Planning," *Policy Sciences* 4, no. 2 (1973), 155-169.

[28] John Doble and Iara Peng, *The Enduring Effects of National Issues Forums (NIF) on High School Students*, unpublished report to the Kettering Foundation (1999).

[29] Ibid, 49.

[30] Katy Jean Harriger and Jill J. McMillan, *Speaking of Politics: Preparing College Students for Democratic Citizenship through Deliberative Dialogue* (Kettering Foundation Press, 2007).

[31] Maria Henson, "The Making of Future Citizens," *Wake Forest Magazine* (Fall 2016) and Katy Harriger, et al., *The Long-Term Impact of Learning to Deliberate: A Follow-up Study of Democracy Fellows and a Class Cohort*, www.kettering.org/catalog/product/long-term-impact (accessed May 30, 2017).

[32] Bill Bishop, *The Big Sort: Why the Clustering of Like-Minded America Is Tearing Us Apart* (Boston: Houghton Mifflin, 2009).

[33] Diana C. Mutz, *Hearing the Other Side: Deliberative versus Participatory Democracy* (New York: Cambridge University Press, 2006).

[34] According to research summarized by the Campaign for the Civic Mission of Schools, American schools offer fewer civic-oriented courses than they did in the 1960s. Now, most students receive a single high school course on American government, compared to as many as three courses a generation ago. Civic learning is de-emphasized in many schools due to the effects of high-stakes testing. Seventy percent of teachers, in one study, reported that social studies courses received less emphasis because of pressure for students to perform on statewide math and language arts tests. http://www.civicmissionofschools.org/the-campaign/civic-learning-fact-sheet (accessed October 5, 2016).

[35] Based upon surveys of students attending public schools in different types of communities, Kahne and Middaugh (2008) concluded that nonwhite students were less likely than whites to have access to civic-oriented social studies classes, discuss current events in school, and engage in simulations of democratic procedures as part of their high school experience. Further, students living in affluent communities had greater access to learning experiences that addressed how laws are made, included participation in service activities, and involved exposure to debates and panel discussions in social studies classes (Joseph Kahne and Ellen Middaugh, "High Quality Civic Education: What Is It and Who Gets It?" *Social Education* 72, no. 1 [2008], 34). These conclusions are consistent with other studies that have documented differences in the quality of classroom conversations in schools serving high and low SES students and in urban and suburban communities (Judith L. Pace, "The Complex and Unequal Impact of High Stakes Accountability on Untested Social Studies," *Theory and Research in Social Education* 39, no. 1 [2011], 32-60; and John S. Wills, "Putting the Squeeze on Social Studies: Managing Teaching Dilemmas in Subject Areas Excluded from State Testing," *Teachers College Record* 109, no. 8 [2007], 1980-2046).

Chapter Three

[36] According to state enrollment data, there were 4500 students in the Huntington School District in 2012. Of these, 561 were ELL; 1891 were Latino and 2008 were economically disadvantaged.

[37] Aryn M. Dotterer and Katie Lowe, "Classroom Context, School Engagement, and Academic Achievement in Early Adolescence," *Journal of Youth and Adolescence* 40, no. 12 (2011), 1649-1660 and Gary W. and Lisa M. Dinella, "Continuity and Change in Early School Engagement: Predictive of Children's Achievement Trajectories from First to Eighth Grade?" *Journal of Educational Psychology* 101, no. 1 (2009), 190.

[38] Fred Newmann, ed. "The Significance and Sources of Student Engagement," *Student Engagement and Achievement in American Secondary Schools* (New York: Teachers College Press, 1992).

[39] Chin R. Reyes, et al., "Classroom Emotional Climate, Student Engagement, and Academic Achievement," *Journal of Educational Psychology* 104, no. 3 (2012), 700.

[40] John T. Guthrie and Marcia H. Davis, "Motivating Struggling Readers in Middle School Through an Engagement Model of Classroom Practice," *Reading and Writing Quarterly* 19, no. 1 (2003), 59-85.

[41] Allan Wigfield, et al., "Development of Achievement Motivation," in *Child and Adolescent Development: An Advanced Course*, edited by William Damon and Richard M. Lerner (Hoboken, NJ: John Wiley and Sons, 2008), 406-434.

[42] Fred M. Newmann, "A Test of Higher-Order Thinking in Social Studies: Persuasive Writing on Constitutional Issues Using the NAEP Approach," *Social Education* 54, no. 6 (1990), 369–373.

[43] Carole L. Hahn, *Becoming Political: Comparative Perspectives on Citizenship Education* (Albany, NY: State University of New York Press, 1997).

[44] For more information about teaching practices that inhibit and support critical thinking and deliberation about controversial issues in the classroom, see Diana E. Hess, *Controversy in the Classroom: The Democratic Power of Discussion* (New York: Routledge, 2009).

[45] David Mathews, *For Communities to Work* (Dayton, OH: Kettering Foundation Press, 2002).

[46] Issue guides are fully developed resources that include issue frameworks as well as relevant facts, information, and context. Issue frameworks are a skeleton or grid that depicts the options/approaches, possible actions, consequences, and trade-offs.

[47] For more information about issue framing and its importance in citizens' terms, see David Mathews, *Naming and Framing Difficult Issues to Make Sound Decisions: A Cousins Research Group Report on Democratic Practices* (Dayton, OH: Kettering Foundation, 2016).

[48] Ibid.

[49] Carol Lee Pyfer, an English language arts teacher in the School District of Lancaster, Pennsylvania, used the term "instigating experiences" in a report to the Kettering Foundation on her experiences with NIF in the classroom. Other teachers reported that they used content in similar ways to increase students' interest in public issues that were unfamiliar to students, or that seemed remote to them.

[50] Mathews, *For Communities to Work*.

[51] Joseph Renzulli, Marcia Gentry, and Sally M. Reis, "A Time and a Place for Authentic Learning," *Educational Leadership* 62, no. 1 (2004), 73.

[52] Laura Greenstein, "Beyond the Core: Assessing Authentic 21st Century Skills," *Principal Leadership* 13, no.4 (2012), 36-42.

[53] The term "differentiated instruction" refers to the process of planning, adapting, and extending learning activities to ensure that they meet the educational needs of diverse learners—often learners who are reading below or above grade level.

[54] Carol Ann Tomlinson, *Differentiated Classroom: Responding to the Needs of All Learners* (Alexandria, VA: ASCD, 2014).

Chapter Four

[55] According to the 2012 Birmingham School District annual report, there were a total of 24,976 students in the school district, of which 23,651 were black.

[56] Julia B. Isaacs, *Economic Mobility of Black and White Families* (Washington: The Pew Charitable Trusts/Brookings Institution, 2007).

[57] James J. Heckman and Paul A. LaFontaine, "The American High School Graduation Rate: Trends and Levels," *The Review of Economics and Statistics* 92, no. 2 (2010), 244-262.

[58] David Mathews, *For Communities to Work.*

[59] Brad Rourke, *Developing Materials for Deliberative Forums* (Dayton, OH: Kettering Foundation, 2014), https://www.kettering.org/wp-content/uploads/Developing-Materials-guide.pdf (accessed December 5, 2016).

[60] Jean E. Rhodes, "Older and Wiser: Mentoring Relationships in Childhood and Adolescence," *Journal of Primary Prevention* 14, no. 3 (1994), 187–196.

Chapter Five

[61] A 2008 study conducted by the National Corporation for Community Service estimated that 60 percent of US elementary schools recognize students' participation in community service, while 51 percent arrange service opportunities for students. See Kimberly Spring, Robert Grimm, Jr., and Nathan Dietz, *Community Service and Service-Learning in America's Schools*, 2008, http://files.eric.ed.gov/fulltext/ED506728.pdf (accessed October 5, 2016).

[62] Shelley Billig, "Research on K-12 School-Based Service-Learning: The Evidence Builds," *Phi Delta Kappan* 81, no. 9 (2000), 658-663.

[63] Richard M. Battistoni, "Service Learning and Democratic Citizenship," *Theory Into Practice* 36, no. 3 (1997), 150-156.

[64] Kaya Yilmaz, "Historical Empathy and Its Implications for Classroom Practices in Schools," *History Teacher* 40, no. 3 (2007), 331-337.

[65] A broader framing of students' PE concern, which would introduce more complex ideas and perspectives, might address the question, how should schools be structured to support optimal youth development?

[66] David Mathews, *For Communities to Work.*

Chapter Six

[67] For more information about NIF Teachers Institutes, go to https://www.nifi.org/en/educators-center (accessed December 5, 2016).

[68]Diana E. Hess, *Controversy in the Classroom*; Diana E. Hess and Paula McAvoy, *The Political Classroom: Evidence and Ethics in Democratic Education* (New York: Routledge, 2014); Walter C. Parker and Diana Hess, "Teaching With and For Discussion," *Teaching and Teacher Education* 17 (2001), 273-289.

[69] Chris McCauley was the director of the David Mathews Center for Civic Life from 2009 to 2015. During that time, the center became a partner with the Birmingham Teachers Institute.

[70] The issue guide on bullying developed by the David Mathews Center for Civic Life is available online at https://mathewscenter.org/wp-content/uploads/2010/12/Bully-Brochure_press_PMS.pdf (accessed December 5, 2016).

[71] The issue guide developed to commemorate the Selma march is available online at http://mathewscenter.org/wp-content/uploads/2014/09/DMC-ProjectC-Singlepgs.pdf. Additional resources are provided by Alabama Public Television to support classroom learning, http://www.aptv.org/IQLEARNING/ElectronicFieldTrips/series.asp?seriesid=3 (accessed December 5, 2016).

Afterword

[72] Kim Pearce, *The Use of CosmoKidz in K-2 Classes in Oracle, Arizona, to Help Children Develop the Social Skills Needed for Effective Citizenship* (Dayton, OH: Final Report to the Kettering Foundation, June 2016).

Bibliography

Albert, Dustin, and Laurence Steinberg. "Judgment and Decision Making in Adolescence." *Journal of Research on Adolescence* 21, no. 1 (2011): 211-224.

Avery, Patricia G. "Teaching Tolerance: What Research Tells Us." *Social Education* 66, no. 5 (2002): 270-275.

Avery, Patricia G., et al. *The Expanding Deliberating in a Democracy (Did) Project Evaluation Report: Year 1 Project Narrative,* http://www.did.deliberating.org/about_us/documents/Expanding%20DID%20Year%201%20(07-08)%20Evaluation.pdf (accessed December 6, 2016).

Battistoni, Richard M. "Service Learning and Democratic Citizenship." *Theory Into Practice* 36, no. 3 (1997): 150-156.

Benali, Abdelkader. "From Teenage Angst to Jihad." *New York Times* (January 13, 2015), http://www.nytimes.com/2015/01/14/opinion/the-anger-of-europes-young-marginalized-muslims.html?_r=0 (accessed October 3, 2016).

Billig, Shelley. "Research on K-12 School-Based Service-Learning: The Evidence Builds." *Phi Delta Kappan* 81, no. 9 (2000): 658-663.

Bishop, Bill. *The Big Sort: Why the Clustering of Like-Minded America Is Tearing Us Apart.* Boston: Houghton Mifflin, 2009.

Bitter, Catherine, Jennifer O'Day, Paul Gubbins, and Miguel Socias. "What Works to Improve Student Literacy Achievement? An Examination of Instructional Practices in a Balanced Literacy Approach." *Journal of Education for Students Placed at Risk* 14, no. 1 (2009): 17-44.

Boyte, Harry, and Nancy N. Kari. *Building America: The Democratic Promise of Public Work.* Philadelphia: Temple University Press, 1996.

Brackett, Mark A., Susan E. Rivers, and Peter Salovey. "Emotional Intelligence: Implications for Personal, Social, Academic, and Workplace Success." *Social and Personality Psychology Compass* 5, no. 1 (2011): 88-103.

Cobb-Clark, Deborah, and Michele Tan. "Noncognitive Skills, Occupational Attainment, and Relative Wages." *Labour Economics* 18, no. 1 (2011): 1-13.

Cohn, Nate. "Polarization Is Dividing American Society, Not Just Politics." *New York Times* (June 12, 2014).

Costa, Arthur L., and Bena Kallick, eds. *Learning and Leading with Habits of Mind: 16 Essential Characteristics for Success.* Alexandria, VA: Association for Supervision and Curriculum Development, 2008.

Cotton, Deborah. "Teaching Controversial Environmental Issues: Neutrality and Balance in the Reality of the Classroom." *Educational Research* 48, no. 2 (2006): 223-224.

David, Tom, Martin Frost, Richard Cohen, and David Eisenhower. *The Partisan Divide.* Campbell, CA: FastPencil Premiere, 2014.

Dinella, Gary W., and Lisa M. Dinella. "Continuity and Change in Early School Engagement: Predictive of Children's Achievement Trajectories from First to Eighth Grade?" *Journal of Educational Psychology* 101, no. 1 (2009): 190.

Doble, John, and Iara Peng. *The Enduring Effects of National Issues Forums (NIF) on High School Students.* Unpublished report to the Kettering Foundation (1999).

Doherty, Joni. *Individual and Community: Deliberative Practices in a First-Year Seminar.* Kettering Foundation (2004), https://www.kettering.org/sites/default/files/product-downloads/JoniDohertyIndividual_0.pdf (accessed October 3, 2016).

Dotterer, Aryn M., and Katie Lowe. "Classroom Context, School Engagement, and Academic Achievement in Early Adolescence." *Journal of Youth and Adolescence* 40, no. 12 (2011): 1649-1660.

Duckworth, Angela L., Christopher Peterson, Michael Matthews, and Dennis Kelly. "Grit: Perseverance and Passion for Long-Term Goals." *Journal of Personality and Social Psychology* 92, no. 6 (2007): 1087.

Durlak, Joseph, et al. "The Impact of Enhancing Students' Social and Emotional Learning: A Meta Analysis of School Based Universal Interventions." *Child Development* 82, no. 1 (2011): 405-432.

Goleman, Daniel. *Emotional Intelligence* (10th Anniversary Hardcover Edition). New York: Bantam, 2006.

Gould, Jonathan, ed. *Guardian of Democracy: The Civic Mission of Schools.* The Leonore Annenberg Institute for Civics of the Annenberg Public Policy Center at the University of Pennsylvania and the Campaign for the Civic Mission of Schools, http://civicmission.s3.amazonaws.com/118/f0/5/171/1/Guardian-of-Democracy-report.pdf (accessed October 3, 2016).

Greenstein, Laura. "Beyond the Core: Assessing Authentic 21st Century Skills." *Principal Leadership* 13, no.4 (2012): 36-42.

Guthrie, John T., and Marcia H. Davis. "Motivating Struggling Readers in Middle School Through an Engagement Model of Classroom Practice." *Reading & Writing Quarterly* 19, no. 1 (2003): 59-85.

Gutmann, Amy, and Dennis Thompson. *Why Deliberative Democracy?* Princeton, NJ: Princeton University Press, 2004.

Hahn, Carole, and Cynthia Tocci. "Classroom Climate and Controverial Issues Discussions: A Five Nation Study." *Theory and Research in Social Education* 18, no. 4 (1990): 344-362.

Hahn, Carole L. *Becoming Political: Comparative Perspectives on Citizenship Education.* Albany, NY: State University of New York Press, 1997.

Harriger, Katy Jean, and Jill J. McMillan. *Speaking of Politics: Preparing College Students for Democratic Citizenship through Deliberative Dialogue.* Dayton, OH: Kettering Foundation Press, 2007.

Harriger, Katy, et al. *The Long-Term Impact of Learning to Deliberate: A Follow-up Study of Democracy Fellows and a Class Cohort.* Dayton, OH: Kettering Foundation Press, 2017.

Hascher, Tina, and Gerda Hagenauer. "Alienation from School." *International Journal of Educational Research* 49, no. 6 (2010): 220-232.

Heckman, James J., and Paul A. LaFontaine. "The American High School Graduation Rate: Trends and Levels." *The Review of Economics and Statistics* 92, no. 2 (2010): 244-262.

Heckman, James J., and Yona Rubinstein. "The Importance of Noncognitive Skills: Lessons from the GED Testing Program," *American Economic Review* 19, no. 2 (2001): 145-149.

Henson, Maria. "The Making of Future Citizens." *Wake Forest Magazine* (Fall 2016).

Hess, Diana E. *Controversy in the Classroom: The Democratic Power of Discussion.* New York: Routledge, 2009.

Hess, Diana E., and Paula McAvoy. *The Political Classroom: Evidence and Ethics in Democratic Education.* New York: Routledge, 2014.

Howell, Penny, Shelley Thomas, and Yuliya Ardasheva. "Talk in the Classroom: Meeting the Developmental, Academic, and Cultural Needs of Middle School Students." *Middle Grades Research Journal* 6, no. 1 (2011): 47-63.

Isaacs, Julia B. *Economic Mobility of Black and White Families.* Washington: The Pew Charitable Trusts/Brookings Institution, 2007.

Jensen, Eric. "How Poverty Affects Classroom Engagement." *Educational Leadership* 70, no. 8 (2013): 24-30.

Kahne, Joseph, and Ellen Middaugh. "High Quality Civic Education: What Is It and Who Gets It?" *Social Education* 72, no. 1 (2008): 34.

Legault, Lisa, Isabelle Green-Demers, and Luc Pelletier. "Why Do High School Students Lack Motivation in the Classroom?" *Journal of Educational Psychology* 98, no. 3 (2006): 567.

Mathews, David. *For Communities to Work.* Dayton, OH: Kettering Foundation Press, 2004.

Mathews, David. *Naming and Framing Difficult Issues to Make Sound Decisions: A Cousins Research Group Report on Democratic Practices.* Dayton, OH: Kettering Foundation, 2016.

135

Meisinger, Elizabeth, et al. "Interaction Quality During Partner Reading." *Journal of Literacy Research* 36, no. 2 (2004): 111-140.

Michaels, Sarah, Catherine O'Connor, and Lauren Resnick. "Deliberative Discourse Idealized and Realized: Accountable Talk in the Classroom and in Civic Life." *Studies in Philosophy and Education* 27, no. 4 (2008): 283-297.

Michaels, Sarah, Richard Sohmer, and Mary C. O'Connor. "Discourse in the Classroom." In *Sociolinguistics: An International Handbook of the Science of Language and Society*, 2nd edition, Herausgegeben von Ulrich Ammon, et al., eds. New York: Walter de Gruyter, 2004.

Mutz, Diana C. *Hearing the Other Side: Deliberative versus Participatory Democracy.* New York: Cambridge University Press, 2006.

National Council for the Social Studies (NCSS). *The College, Career, and Civic Life (C3) Framework for Social Studies State Standards: Guidance for Enhancing the Rigor of K-12 Civics, Economics, Geography, and History.* Silver Spring, MD: NCSS, 2013. http://www.socialstudies.org/system/files/c3/C3-Framework-for-Social-Studies.pdf (accessed October 3, 2016).

Newmann, Fred, ed. "The Significance and Sources of Student Engagement." *Student Engagement and Achievement in American Secondary Schools.* New York: Teachers College Press, 1992.

Newmann, Fred M. "A Test of Higher-Order Thinking in Social Studies: Persuasive Writing on Constitutional Issues Using the NAEP Approach." *Social Education* 54, no. 6 (1990): 369-373.

Pace, Judith L. "The Complex and Unequal Impact of High Stakes Accountability on Untested Social Studies." *Theory & Research in Social Education* 39, no. 1 (2011): 32-60.

Parker, Walter C., and Diana Hess. "Teaching With and For Discussion." *Teaching and Teacher Education* 17 (2001): 273-289.

Payton, John W., et al. "Social and Emotional Learning: A Framework for Promoting Mental Health and Reducing Risk Behavior in Children and Youth." *Journal of School Health* 70, no. 5 (2000): 179-185.

Pearce, Kim. *The Use of CosmoKidz in K-2 Classes in Oracle, Arizona, to Help Children Develop the Social Skills Needed for Effective Citizenship.* Dayton, OH: Final Report to the Kettering Foundation, June 2016.

Porter-O'Donnell, Carol. "Beyond the Yellow Highlighter: Teaching Annotation Skills to Improve Reading Comprehension." *English Journal* 93, no. 5 (May 2004): 82-89.

Renzulli, Joseph, Marcia Gentry, and Sally M. Reis. "A Time and a Place for Authentic Learning." *Educational Leadership* 62, no. 1 (2004): 73.

Reyes, Chin R., et al. "Classroom Emotional Climate, Student Engagement, and Academic Achievement." *Journal of Educational Psychology* 104, no. 3 (2012): 700.

Rhodes, Jean E. "Older and Wiser: Mentoring Relationships in Childhood and Adolescence." *Journal of Primary Prevention* 14, no. 3 (1994): 187-196.

Rittel, Horst W. J., and Melvin M. Webber. "Dilemmas in a General Theory of Planning." *Policy Sciences* 4, no. 2 (1973): 155-169.

Rourke, Brad. *Developing Materials for Deliberative Forums.* Dayton, OH: Kettering Foundation, 2014, https://www.kettering.org/wp-content/uploads/Developing-Materials-guide.pdf (accessed December 5, 2016).

Spring, Kimberly, Robert Grimm, Jr., and Nathan Dietz. *Community Service and Service-Learning in America's Schools.* Washington: Corporation for National and Community Service, Office of Research and Policy Development, 2008, http://files.eric.ed.gov/fulltext/ED506728.pdf (accessed October 5, 2016).

Tomlinson, Carol Ann. *Differentiated Classroom: Responding to the Needs of All Learners.* Alexandria, VA: ASCD, 2014.

Tough, Paul. *How Children Succeed: Grit, Curiosity, and the Hidden Power of Character.* New York: First Mariner Books, 2013.

Wigfield, Allan, et al. "Development of Achievement Motivation." In *Child and Adolescent Development: An Advanced Course,* edited by William Damon and Richard M. Lerner. Hoboken, NJ: John Wiley and Sons, 2008: 406-434.

Williams, Kipling, Joseph Forgas, and William von Hippel, eds. *The Social Outcast: Ostracism, Social Exclusion, Rejection, and Bullying.* New York: Psychology Press, 2005.

Wills, John S. "Putting the Squeeze on Social Studies: Managing Teaching Dilemmas in Subject Areas Excluded from State Testing." *Teachers College Record* 109, no. 8 (2007): 1980-2046.

Yilmaz, Kaya. "Historical Empathy and Its Implications for Classroom Practices in Schools." *History Teacher* 40, no. 3 (2007): 331-337.